God Will Never Violate Your Free Will

Mission: To Proclaim Transformation and Truth
Publisher: Transformed Publishing, Cocoa, FL
Website: www.transformedpublishing.com
Email: transformedpublishing@gmail.com

ISBN: 978-1-953241-75-7

God Will Never Violate Your Free Will

Jacque

Table of Contents

Preface

There is a cultural assault going on. This book is about *that* war and *those* roots which we struggle with on a daily basis.

Our brains instruct our bodies. The mind guides the soul. Our heart is the most vital organ in the body. It keeps the blood flowing. It is the organ that keeps us alive. It stops pumping, we stop breathing soon after.

> " 'For here's what I'm going to do: I'm going to take you out of these countries, gather you from all over, and bring you back to your own land. I'll pour pure water over you and scrub you clean. I'll give you a new heart, put a new spirit in you. I'll remove the stone heart from your body and replace it with a heart that's God-willed, not self-willed. I'll put my Spirit in you and make it possible for you to do what I tell you and live by my commands. You'll once again live in the land I gave your ancestors. You'll be My people! I'll be your God![' ")
> -Ezekiel 36:24-28 MSG

A promised land, the promised land, is the place of freedom. When we are living in unity and like-mindedness with our Heavenly Father. This "land" [ground; soil] represents the heart. Promised means engaged by Word or writing; stipulated. Stipulation is the act of agreeing, an agreement. Stipulation: agreed; contracted; covenanted.

Each and every one of us are invaluable. Let's not allow "cultural" standards to make us think otherwise!

One Sabbath as He was teaching in a synagogue, He saw a seriously handicapped woman who had been bent double for eighteen years and was unable to straighten herself.

Calling her over to Him, Jesus said, "Woman, you are healed of your sickness!" He touched her, and instantly she could stand straight. How she praised and thanked God!

-Luke 13:10-13

This "lady in the church" was bent over [sickened by a stronghold] for eighteen years and "the building" had not fixed her. There are multiple ways satan and his band of demons bring influence into our lives which hold us hostage to strongholds [lies that we believe in our hearts, therefore truths to us]. Relationship with our Creator can, if we allow it, set us free from a stronghold sickness; instantly. God, Adonai, Yahweh, will NOT violate our free will!

Most people spend their entire lives looking for love and acceptance and security and peace of mind. Yet, just as I did, they reject God's offering of all that, plus so much more! That searching, our searching, leads us down the roads of life—the paths of good and evil; the heartaches and the adventures. Our individual journeys. Our stories! And, eventually, our legacies.

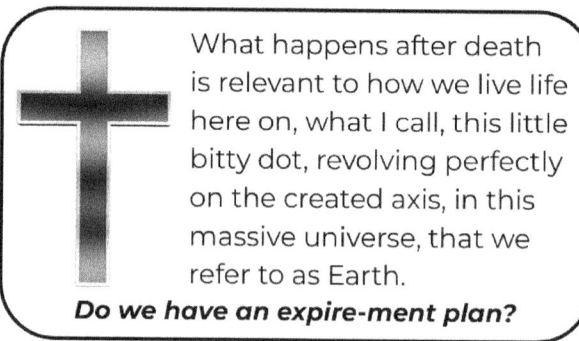

What happens after death is relevant to how we live life here on, what I call, this little bitty dot, revolving perfectly on the created axis, in this massive universe, that we refer to as Earth.
Do we have an expire-ment plan?

> Without wise leadership, a nation is in trouble; but with good counselors there is safety.
>
> -Proverbs 11:14

Without good direction, people lose their way. Too many people, too many "Christians", the all too many whosoevers, spend life in that area of heartache and pain—as if a real-life heart surgery was performed, with the broken ribs and everything, never getting to experience the healing and the joy that comes with the acceptance of the Holy Spirit, the One given to us by God through His precious Son, Jesus Christ, Yeshua, the last Adam, who, through His blood, through His sacrifice and resurrection reconciled us with God.

When our physical heart is inefficient, in other words, not working properly, as it is intended to do, it limits every part of our lives. Our strength. Our mobility. Everything. This one little organ, located at the center of our being, functioning properly or improperly!

Here is Truth that our Heavenly Father would like for us to know: If our spiritual heart is not healthy, if we are not healthy at the center of our being, spiritually, it diminishes every aspect of our lives!

The Scripture, "as a man thinketh in his heart, so is he" (see Proverbs 23:7) is simply a true statement, a fact, a black and white philosophy, an absolute, that if we believe something to be true or false, in the core of our being, it is true or false "to us", "to you", "to me"!

> Watch out for people who try to dazzle you with big words and intellectual double-talk. They want to drag you off into endless arguments that never amount to

anything. They spread their ideas through the empty traditions of human beings and the empty superstitions of spirit beings. But that's not the way of Christ. Everything of God gets expressed in him, so you can see and hear him clearly. You don't need a telescope, a microscope, or a horoscope to realize the fullness of Christ, and the emptiness of the universe without him. When you come to him, that fullness comes together for you, too. His power extends over everything.

-Colossians 2:8-10 MSG

When we are NOT listening to The Highest Ruler, who lives inside of us [disciples of Yeshua], who are we listening to? I am seriously thinking right now about that devil on one shoulder story except now, I see it ain't really just a story!

Thank you for acquiring this book! Please know everything in it is written out of love. In these pages, you are going to see Truth backed up in Scripture from four translations of the Word of God. Most Scripture quotations are taken from *The Living Bible, Paraphrased.*

I encourage you to make the time to look up each Scripture in your Bible, meditate on them, and get them rooted deep down in your heart. I also encourage people who are dealing with something to look up God's promise regarding that stronghold, write it down, fold the piece of paper up, then put the promise in their shoe and stand on it! If we stick to the processes necessary for healing that sickness, we will be healed from that sickness. Our God is a Promise Keeper! God never starts something He doesn't finish. Humans do that.

This book is written in the Southern-style, Southern dialect, of my real / true / authentic person. Please take the slang and punctuations light-heartedly, AND, with the exception of direct quotations from copywritten Scripture, the capital-ization of "He, Him, Himself" plus lower-case "satan" seriously. It is most certainly my intent to give respect where respect is due.

In all Scripture, it is imperative we discover the context of the Word / Verse / Paragraph. The "war" I am referencing, the "open heart surgery" I am referring to, has to do with our entire "heart". Sometimes this heart is our mind, our thoughts. Sometimes it may be the heart itself. For example, God gave Solomon "largeness of heart" in 1 Kings, Chapter 4, and Verse 29. In this particular context, Scripture is speaking of the mind. In Romans 7:25, the blood-pumping heart. Other mentions are referring to the heart / soul / mind; a combination of intellect, will, thought-processing, decisions, emotions. As you consume this book and God's Word, please study the context in order to separate and/or combine the spirit man, the mind, the heart, versus the "flesh", the physical mankind. What I have come to know in my continuing education in God's Word, is that a renewal of the heart, of the mind, of the soul [versus riding the rollercoaster life of emotional and programmed thinking] is most certainly crucial should one desire to have the victorious and abundant lifestyle the Father, the Son, and the Holy Spirit intended from the exact moment of CREATION.

✝

Acknowledgements

Many thanks go out to the following disciples of Christ who allow the Spirit of the Lord to use them in a mighty way. Without their influence and discipleship, this book would not have come together as it is. Now, I am also a willing vessel of our precious Jesus Christ, in the process of renewing my mind, with the deep desire to build upon the Kingdom!

Andrew Wommack (awmi.net)

Allen Jackson Ministries (AllenJackson.com)

Dr. Tony Evans, The Urban Alternative (tonyevans.org)

Dr. David Jeremiah (DavidJeremiah.org)

Joyce Meyer Ministries (JoyceMeyer.org)

Pastor Don Adkins, Christ Central Church

Diana Robinson, Transformed Publishing
(transformedpublishing.com)

Steven Furtick Ministries (StevenFurtick.com)

Trinity Broadcasting Network (tbn.org)

Chapter 1
Are We Listening

Have you ever really thought about how we, how people, label? I mean *really* thought about it!?! It is done every second of every day. It is an envious, deceitful, almost unavoidable, demonic source of strife that has been around since the age ... well, since the age of satan. One of the worst forms of labeling, which probably causes the whole trickle-down effect, is the way we label ourselves! satan's stomping ground! Right inside of our own heads. And here we are, with over 8 billion heads in the world. That is a whole lot of territory. Why in the world are we so loyal to labeling? Wonder what would happen if we were to be *that* loyal to what God says about us!

The Bible tells us that we become what we believe. Many Christians, unfortunately, label themselves "subpar". What an awesome stomping ground the devil has access to! Over 8 billion spirits, on this teeny tiny dot, smaller than the size of a marble [in comparison to the universe], planet we call earth. And again, a root of the spiritual battle, is that we want all 8 billion of these people to like us; to accept us.

That brings us to this, God's message, through me, to us— there is a cultural assault goin' on.

Spiritual conflict and spiritual warfare are the story of Scripture. Today, deception runs rampant and is tolerated because it is intertwined into free speech. Here, in the United States, even. It is so very important that we know the

Scriptures so we know what God, the Creator of the dot, is doing here on the planet earth.

The word peace can be defined as a place of quiet and tranquility. We all see, physically and spiritually, saved or not saved, that peace is not the constant state of our culture this day, nor back in the day. Yet, Yeshua says we can have it. So, what does that mean?

Another definition of peace is a state of security. Like feeling secure in our homes or secure in our relationships. Jesus states, in our Survival Guide, that we, out of free will, can have peace. That He would leave us His peace. That we could live within His love, and have, maintain, experience, peace.

> ["]But when the Father sends the Comforter instead of me—and by Comforter I mean the Holy Spirit—he will teach you much, as well as remind you of everything I myself have told you.
>
> "I am leaving you with a gift—peace of mind and heart! And the peace I give isn't fragile like the peace the world gives. So don't be troubled or afraid."
>
> -John 14:26-27

It is a fact, it is written, that Jesus did not lead a life of quietness and tranquility. Most everywhere He went, He was rejected and ridiculed. So, there goes cultural relationship security right out the window. Wonder how He labeled himself?

> ["]Remember what I told you—I am going away, but I will come back to you again. If you really love me, you will be very happy for me, for now I can go to the Father, who is greater than I am. I have told you these things

before they happen so that when they do, you will believe in me.

"I don't have much more time to talk to you, for the evil prince of this world approaches. He has no power over me, but I will freely do what the Father requires of me so that the world will know that I love the Father. Come, let's be going."

-John 14:28-31

he [the evil prince of this world] has NO POWER over me! I live in love, in the Vine! Our Father is the Gardener! Peace on this planet, the physical, dictionary peace, is not going to happen on this dot, in this culture, without Jesus. This is why our purpose is to shine while we patiently, peacefully, passionately, wait on Jesus' return, in the love of the Father, the Gardener of the dot, the Overseer of the Christian. When we think of peace, tranquility, spiritually, we are to be thinking of calming the wind and the waves without angst, no anxiety in the mind and heart.

Let's look at a couple of examples of how Jesus, who told us, who tells us in the Scriptures, handled some cultural storms during His walk here on the dot—storms the evil prince of this world was and is going to stir up in the culture.

One, He is not anxious about disease, DIS EASE, of any kind, because He can bring the dead to life again. Two, He is not anxious about how to feed the multitude, the children of God who are lacking in something they need, because He knows the Father owns The Bread of Life. He is not anxious about politicians who are threatening Him with evil because He knows the Father is the One with all authority and the Father has invested in Him, in us. I ask: Do we know that? Do we believe that? Are we anxious for nothing or for just about everything!?!

Where do we get our strength? Our bank account? Our social media likes? Which political party is "running the nation"?

If you are expecting peace, strength, and security from the news, I bet you are tired, exhausted even. We are subject to a great deal of anxiety every day. From where are you eating? Maybe some of us enjoy the turmoil so we can go around complaining about it, murmuring, circling the mountain for 40 years. I submit to you, that as long as our names are recorded, He knows the hairs on our heads! Do not get caught up in culture. He is watching over us!

Peace, strength, security, in the midst of conflict, is very much a possibility—a gift! It is a peace, the peace, we are going to need in order to get to be in the place God has called us to. Living in HIS Love, while we do life here on this dot.

> "Then the people begged for a king, and God gave them Saul (son of Kish), a man of the tribe of Benjamin, who reigned for forty years. But God removed him and replaced him with David as king, a man about whom God said, 'David (son of Jesse) is a man after my own heart, for he will obey me'. And it is one of King David's descendants, Jesus, who is God's promised Savior of Israel!["]
>
> -Acts 13:21-23

Linda ... after My own heart. Melissa ... after My own heart. Oliver ... after My own heart. She / he obeys Me ... just goes around and does whatever I ask them to do. *Are we listening?*

These are the last words of David: "David, the son of Jesse, speaks. David, the man to whom God gave such wonderful success; David, the anointed of the God of Jacob; David, sweet psalmist of Israel: The Spirit of the Lord spoke by me, and his word was on my tongue. The Rock of Israel said to me: 'One shall come who rules righteously, who rules in the fear of God. He shall be as the light of the morning; a cloudless sunrise when the tender grass springs forth upon the earth; as sunshine after rain.' And it is my family He has chosen! Yes, God has made an everlasting covenant with me; His agreement is eternal, final, sealed. He will constantly look after my safety and success."

-2 Samuel 23:1-5

Do we realize our value? Really? Do we "walk" with God? Do life with God? Are you growing weary?

I promise you when God says "all", He means "all". Until I came to that realization, that revelation, I was not only weary, I was lost! Dead! At this point in my life, and after being backslidden for so many years, I find myself in a constant state of learning to listen—passionately listen. Finding myself falling further and further from the state of panic, into His arms of peace and joy and love and kindness. Into the understanding of my value, my covenant with God. It is a process. And it takes time and patience and faithfulness and Holy Spirit control. There is a difference between diligence and simply having a desire, same as peace and conflict!

As David emphasized in Verse 5: Is our house right with God? At the end of his life, the last words he speaks magnify his covenant with God. Eternal. Final. Sealed. Do we believe that our covenant with God is arranged and secured in every part?

All parts? Constantly recognizing, reorganizing, and reprioritizing our priorities? Or, are some of us stuck in a story of being a little perturbed at God because He is not giving us everything we want? There is not one Verse, in the whole Bible, where God promises to give us everything we want.

> And let steadfastness have its full effect, that you may be perfect and complete, lacking in nothing.
> -James 1:4 ESV

Steadfast. Diligence. Lacking in nothing. That is our promise from God! David, a warrior, moved from killing lions and bears to giants. Almost the entire Chapter of 2 Samuel 23, David recited the mighty men who served with him. Wonder why?

The heroes we know from Scripture did not lead their lives apart from cultural conflict wrapped in a blanket of peace. They were secure in their relationship with the Father of Abraham, the Father of the heavens and of the earth. And we now have the gift of the Holy Spirit dwelling within us!

> So roll up your sleeves, get your head in the game, be totally ready to receive the gift that's coming when Jesus arrives. Don't lazily slip back into those old grooves of evil, doing just what you feel like doing. You didn't know any better then; you do now. As obedient children, let yourselves be pulled into a way of life shaped by God's life, a life energetic and blazing with holiness. God said, "I am holy; you be holy."
> -1 Peter 1:13-16 MSG

Let's prepare our minds for action!

Friends, when life gets really difficult, don't jump to the conclusion that God isn't on the job. Instead, be glad that you are in the very thick of what Christ experienced. This is a spiritual refining process, with glory just around the corner.

If you're abused because of Christ, count yourself fortunate. It's the Spirit of God and his glory in you that brought you to the notice of others. If they're on you because you broke the law or disturbed the peace, that's a different matter. But if it's because you're a Christian, don't give it a second thought. Be proud of the distinguished status reflected in that name!

It's judgment time for God's own family. We're first in line. If it starts with us, think what it's going to be like for those who refuse God's Message!

                                                    -1 Peter 4:12-18 MSG

Our glory is just around the corner! Why are we even surprised? We are in a spiritual refining process. It's judgment time for the people of God. We all face points of vulnerability!

Last of all I want to remind you that your strength must come from the Lord's mighty power within you. Put on all of God's armor so that you will be able to stand safe against all strategies and tricks of Satan. For we are not fighting against people made of flesh and blood, but against persons without bodies—the evil rulers of the unseen world, those mighty satanic beings and great evil princes of darkness who rule this world; and against huge number of wicked spirits in the spirit world.

                                                    -Ephesians 6:10-12

God is strong, and He wants us to be strong. Do we armor up every morning? Let's not be caught off guard. We need to be actively engaged in Yeshua's return. God is the God of the angel armies, a Warrior, a Triumphant King. Not knowing or hiding from this Truth, or any Truth, does not diminish Truth. Let's live in His victory! We are in spiritual warfare! And, for the most part, a lot of people tend to put all the blame on the culture; it has gotta be somebody's fault, *right*! Once again, the Bible reads:

> For we do not wrestle against flesh and blood, but against the rulers, against the authorities, against the cosmic powers over this present darkness, against the spiritual forces of evil in the heavenly places.
> -Ephesians 6:12 ESV

Not just on this dot, with the over 8 billion flesh and bloods. Hiding doesn't help.

Question: Do we really think that the Creator of the heavens and the earth would send His Son, a very part of Himself, to this dot, to humble Himself, for the incarnation, for the act of assuming flesh, to be obedient ALL the way to the brutal, humiliating, painful death of crucifixion, for our benefit, for us to then NOT label ourselves as His?

"Oh, but Jacque, I was just counting on accepting Jesus and the Bible story as true, living my life 'trying' not to sin, then takin' my ticket to heaven."

Okee-dokee then. Blending in with the culture is not an option. Especially if we desire AND diligently, passionately, seek God's gift of peace. There is a battle goin' on my friends! And God has deployed us, you and me, into the situation, into this generation. We are not here by accident or explosion! Like it or not, believe it or not, the Bible portrays Adonai as Military Commander.

> The Lord is a warrior—yes, Jehovah is his name. He has overthrown Pharaoh's chariots and armies, drowning them in the sea. The famous Egyptian captains are dead beneath the waves.
>
> -Exodus 15:3-4

This is after blood and frogs and lice and flies and other plagues and locusts and darkness without one single ray of light and destroying all the oldest, Egyptian sons plus the firstborn of the animals in Egypt! We may have free will, but God has free reign! Read the Book of Revelation, which reveals Jesus Christ Himself, supporting this fact!

> As Joshua was sizing up the city of Jericho, a man appeared nearby with a drawn sword. Joshua strode over to him and demanded, "Are you friend or foe?"
>
> "I am the Commander-in-Chief of the Lord's army," he replied.
>
> Joshua fell to the ground before him and worshiped him and said, "Give me your commands."
>
> "Take off your shoes," the Commander told him, "for this is holy ground." And Joshua did.
>
> -Joshua 5:13-15

Moses is gone. Joshua has assumed the leadership position. And another angelic being, a messenger from the heavens not of flesh and blood, comes to the dot with a drawn sword and confronts Joshua. Yet another divine encounter recorded in Scripture, this one revealing Himself as military commander.

So again, like it or not, there is a battle, and there is a cultural assault goin' on!

> Hear the tumult on the mountains! Listen as the armies march! It is the tumult and the shout of many nations. The Lord Almighty has brought them here,
>
> -Isaiah 13:4

This Passage references God's judgment on the City of Babylon.

We are to revere *this* Lord God Almighty of war and of love! Without the emotion of fear and with utmost respect. Without understanding His character, we will most certainly be caught off guard regarding His provision for His people! The Lord is our Shepherd (*see* Psalm 23). Are you sitting at the table of Yeshua? Do you label yourself as His child? Cup overflowing?

Rebellion from God does not lead to the road of freedom. It does not lead to the road of victory. It does not lead to the gift of peace that surpasses all understanding. The culture's rebellion reached the point of not accepting male and female as the only genders, contrary to the Word of God, "So God created man in His own image; in the image of God He created him; male and female He created them" (Genesis 1:27). *What in the world is next!?!*

Remember, there is a story in Scripture, even before we get to the story of Adam, that helps us understand the rebellious "my way" nature of the human race! It began in the heavens, not on the dot. It began with an archangel named lucifer who influenced an already existing race of beings, occupying the universe prior to the confrontation in the Garden of Eden (*see*

Isaiah 14 and Revelation 12). The battle of envy and strife and discord was directed toward God, way-prior to satan turning his attention toward Eve!

> So the Lord God said to the serpent, "This is your punishment: You are singled out from among all the domestic and wild animals of the whole earth—to be cursed. You shall grovel in the dust as long as you live, crawling along on your belly. From now on you and the woman will be enemies, as will all your offspring and hers. And I will put the fear of you into the woman, and between your offspring and hers. He shall strike you on your head, while you will strike at his heel."
>
> -Genesis 3:14-15 MSG

God, Adonai, The Mighty Warrior, literally speaking, to satan, in what just very well may be the first prophecy in the Bible of future events, regarding his and the humans' conditioning ... judgment. He told satan that he would strike the heel of a future descendant of Adam & Eve. However, God also states that a future descendant would strike satan's head. In other words, game over. The battle is already won. We are simply in the midst of it.

The focus of our Bible, of our Survival Guide, is God dealing with Adam plus his descendants. Only God knows the complete story of our little dot and what happened within the heavens prior to Him creating this planet. And, if we attempt to explain spiritual things scientifically and/or as complete history, we may weaken our faith, generate confusion, plus lose sight of the focus of our Bible story. The story of the Bible, is for our benefit ... for equipping us to gain a better understanding of the battle. How are you, how am I, how are we, gonna be victorious if we don't know the story? If our heads are crushed, if our minds are boggled, we're out of the game; our hearts are hard; we are living in cultural confusion and chaos. And that is exactly the way satan likes it. If you really think about it, it's pretty simple! satan is succeeding, on this dot, in weakening the human race's desire, determination, diligence to accept God's—the Bible's, invitation to live here, looking forward to there. With God. With Son of Man. With the Holy Spirit guiding us there!

Jesus is the Son of Adam. Yeshua Himself mentions this over and over again in the New Testament. Let's look at the way Paul refers to Jesus:

> The Scriptures tell us that the first man, Adam, was given a natural, human body but Christ is more than that, for He was life-giving Spirit.
>
> -1 Corinthians 15:45

Obviously, Jesus was not the last person to be born from the lineage of Adam. However, Jesus provided atonement for judgment pronounced in Genesis 3:14-15 in response to Adam's rebellion. So, what Paul means is that Adam, in the Garden, was the first of the human race, but the Son of Adam, the Last Adam, Yeshua, was and is a life-giving Spirit! Jesus ended the evil brought upon His race, the beings in heavenly places!

> First, then, we have these human bodies and later on God gives us spiritual, heavenly bodies. Adam was made from the dust of the earth, but Christ came from heaven above. Every human being has a body just like Adam's, made of dust, but all who become Christ's will have the same kind of body as His—a body from

heaven. Just as each of us now has a body like Adam's, so we shall some day have a body like Christ's.

I tell you this, my brothers: an earthly body made of flesh and blood cannot get into God's kingdom. These perishable bodies of ours are not the right kind to live forever. But I am telling you this strange and wonderful secret: we shall not all die, but we shall all be given new bodies! It will all happen in a moment, in the twinkling of an eye, when the last trumpet is blown. For there will be a trumpet blast from the sky, and all the Christians who have died will suddenly become alive, with new bodies that will never, never die; and then we who are still alive shall suddenly have new bodies too. For our earthly bodies, the ones we have now that can die, must be transformed into heavenly bodies that cannot perish but will live forever.

When this happens, then at last this Scripture will come true—"Death is swallowed up in victory." O death, where then your victory? Where then your sting? For sin—the sting that causes death—will all be gone; and the law, which reveals our sins, will no longer be our judge. How we thank God for all of this! It is he who makes us victorious through Jesus Christ our Lord!

So, my dear brothers, since future victory is sure, be strong and steady, always abounding in the Lord's work, for you know that nothing you do for the Lord is ever wasted as it would be if there were no resurrection.

-1 Corinthians 15:46-58

This is true. Believe it or not. We all live forever, spiritually. And, again, we cannot buy a ticket into the heavens. However, Jesus paid it all! Once we accept Him as our Lord and Savior, we are His, and we are to label ourselves as such. Living against the cultural grain. But if we don't understand the assault, we too can be deceived by the craftiness of satan, in our minds, corrupted from the simplicity that is in Christ (*see* 2 Corinthians 11:3).

> But not everyone who hears the Good News has welcomed it, for Isaiah the prophet said, "Lord, who has believed me when I told them?" Yet faith comes from listening to this Good News—the Good News about Christ.
>
> -Romans 10:16-17

Are we hearing only or are we listening? Or are we choosing to allow the serpent, the evil one, and his band of angels to entice us into rebellion? There is NO peace there. Only a short time of play, with ups & downs, like everybody else, then death, and judgment, by Jesus, by the Creator of this little bitty dot, floating, turning and turning in this big ole universe.

We are not playin' some kinda game called Life-and-Done! Let's open our Bibles. Make the time. Hear, really listen, by way of the Holy Spirit, this opportunity extended to us to follow Christ!

Chapter 2
Fruitful & Useful

When Christ identified with us, His created human race, in the incarnation, the act of clothing Himself with flesh, joining us here on the dot in human form with human emotions and human thoughts, human temptations, human hurts, leading a perfect, sinless life; then, choosing to take our sins, past, present, and future, into Himself, suffering in a most inhumane way, for you and for me; He opened the door to a whole new form of existence! A spiritual realm that existed well before this dot we refer to as a planet, existing in a big ole universe that we have yet to begin to explore in its entirety, the one that used to be dark.

> When God began creating the heavens and the earth, the earth was at first a shapeless, chaotic mass, with the Spirit of God brooding over the dark vapors.
> -Genesis 1:1-2

There was plenty happening in this universe prior to the creation of the human race.

> "Where were you when I laid the foundations of the earth? Tell me, if you know so much. Do you know how its dimensions were determined, and who did the surveying? What supports its foundations, and who laid its cornerstone as the morning stars sang together and all the angels shouted for joy?["]
> -Job 38:4-7

Job is presumed to be the first Book written by the human race. Job was quite wealthy and quite rebellious! He questioned God, wondering why he couldn't have everything he wanted; about why things are going differently than he thought; and told the Creator how things would be better "if". And with an audible voice, God answered!

Also, Solomon, the wisest and the wealthiest human being thus far on this dot, a king who built the first Temple, blessed the people of Israel in 2 Chronicles, Chapter 6. Verse 18 reads:

> "But will God indeed dwell with man on the earth? Behold, heaven and the highest heaven cannot contain you, how much less this house that I have built!["]
> -2 Chronicles 6:18 ESV

Humans were NOT FIRST. The people in the Bible are real people with real history in the real world, history books, written by real humans that we can research.

> Then Ezra prayed, "You alone are God. You have made the skies and the heavens, the earth and the seas, and everything in them. You preserve it all; and all the angels of heaven worship you.["]
> -Nehemiah 9:6

Multiple heavens. Multiple beings. One God! One lucifer, who rebelled, and who has access to our lives, as does his army of fallen angels, roaming around, seeking whom they may devour!

Hence, this cultural assault that is going on now, and then. The wheat and the tares must grow together (see Matthew 13:30). Without the Holy Spirit, well, it will be difficult to recognize and stay clear of danger. I am reminded of the catchphrase, "Danger, Will Robinson!"

The Father, and it is written … especially throughout Revelation, extends an invitation to whosoever plus expects His people to follow Christ, to live Christ-like lives in peace, in love … exposing our fruit of His Spirit to our culture. We have purpose! He heeds that we not be stubbornly indifferent! The universe is filled with a multitude of beings, and there is NO reconciliation between good and evil spirits [Jesus' blood reconciles God and humans]. Our journey here is to take our place in the unfolding purposes of God, Adonai, Yahweh, THE CREATOR! To not be simply a part of "the church" building that does "good things" and "religious activities" mimicking civic organizations. To understand that our assignment is to armor up, rise up, and take our stand against all the schemes of the evil one. To prepare our minds for action. If there is no distinction in the way you live, in the way I live, in the way Christians live, our faith is in question! We are engaged in a spiritual battle. Our Survival Guide tells us how to survive it and be victoriously triumphant! Our struggle is not against physical persons, the human race, the worldly culture we were, *we are* assigned to live in. If we are tired and weary, we are not getting our strength, our joy, our peace, from the Word of God!

When we are first saved, repent, and accept Christ as our Lord & Savior, we receive the Seed of God's Divine Nature. God, the Holy Spirit, moves into our soul, our human, our real, self-life in *Seed* form. 2 Peter, Chapter 1, Verse 8, tells us, the more we go on, the more we experience life in time, we are to grow spiritually, grow our faith by way of Verses 2-7. If those qualities, if we claim those qualities and if those qualities are increasing, we become fruitful and useful to God, to our Lord Jesus Christ, Yeshua, the Risen One. Spiritual growth is more of Christ expressing Himself through less of "ME!" For spiritual growth, *that* Incorruptible Seed must develop. A growth process must occur. No commitment, no submission, no true salvation. No renewal of the mind, no dead-man-living. As Verse 9 puts it, "blind indeed." Or at the very least, short-sighted; that human has forgotten God delivered them from the old life of sin so they can live a strong, good life now for the Lord.

So, our choices, deliberate and focused choices, are fruitful or fruitless. Like physical fruit, it bears the character of the tree, the vine, to which it is a part of (apple tree, apples; just as grapevine, grapes). Christians, Christ-like-character! Our responses, our attitudes, our words, our thinking, the people we hang around with, the entertainment we indulge in, the sins we choose to ignore (ya' know, since we are covered by grace), all that, all those, will be in the process of trans-formation to bear the character of the Vine. Another quality of fruit is it is always visible. You can see an orange. You can see a pear. Secret agent Christians are not fruity when they are selective and only come out at night or in church buildings or to particular friends. If a Christian is growing in Christ, abiding in Christ, changing their mind to the way Christ thinks, it should be obvious! Guilty if arrested! Should Christians be arrested for showing themselves as Christian, would you be found guilty in that cultural court of law?

Also, fruit exists for the benefit of another, grown usually for the purpose of eating, consumption; benefit. The opposite is rotting, decaying; not useful. If a Christian spends their whole Christian life on themselves; rotten. People love to pick good, ripe fruit, and take a bite. We should ask ourselves: Is there anyone who wants to take a bite from me, from my life of fruit? Do I draw people to God or push them away? We are blessed when we are blessings; benefiting to one another, part of the family of God, one body, serving God and others! The Word of

God teaches us how to practice the processes necessary to bear fruit that others would like to take a bite out of. To become fishermen of men! So that others will be asking, "How can I become more like you?" Kind, gentle, joyful, patient, good, faithful, loving, peaceful, in control of your emotions and reactions and mouth and thoughts (because we are consulting with the Holy Spirit in all things). It is our choice to become bitter or better! Godly or godless. Sweet or bitter. Ripe or rotten. Helpful or hurtful. Victorious or victim.

Each and every one of us (whosoever) is called into the ministry of Jesus. We do not have to be up on a stage or standing behind a podium in order to influence people and represent Him. Most people live their lives, maybe get married, maybe raise some kids, go to workplaces, clean the house, maintain the lawn, go to the grocery store, visit the dentist, go walking in the park; regular, ordinary life. God's desire is that we do all those things with and for Him while representing Him! The people who need Jesus most are not watching God's representatives on the stage and behind podiums; they are watching us! And we are responsible for how we "preach" without ever even saying a word! 2 Corinthians 2:15 describes Christians as the sweet fragrance of Christ who exhales unto God, the aroma of Christ. That wholesome fragrance of Christ in our lives touches the saved and unsaved all around us, all the time! As does a stench of evil.

> Notice among yourselves, dear brothers, that few of you who follow Christ have big names or power or wealth. Instead, God has deliberately chosen to use ideas the world considers foolish and of little worth in order to shame those people considered by the world as wise and great. He has chosen a plan despised by the world,

counted as nothing at all, and used it to bring down to nothing those the world considers great, so that no one anywhere can ever brag in the presence of God.

-1 Corinthians 1:26-29

For God to flow through us, we must come to the end of ourselves (self, selfish; I am always on my mind; my will be done). Especially when we "feel" like Father is not moving fast enough. Or when we don't "know" the outcome of a situation He put us in or may allow to take place in any given season. Doubt and fear are sure to take over and neither glorify the Lord! God will not share His glory with another. If that statement hardens our hearts, we still have a rebellious spirit that must be worked out in the way we think [our thought processes]. Our minds are the battlefield. No renewal of the mind, no different outcome of the battle for control. The battle of anger or envy or strife. The battle for power and money (fame and fortune). The flesh is weak (*see* Matthew 26:41). All good and perfect things come from God. Including wisdom and power (*see* James 1:16-17).

And because of him you are in Christ Jesus, who became to us wisdom from God, righteousness and sanctification and redemption, so that, as it is written, "Let the one who boasts, boast in the Lord."

-1 Corinthians 1:30-31 ESV

The longer "I" take credit for what I do have and what "I" do without the help of the Holy Spirit, the longer I remain in prison, in chains, bound up in evil. Without God, without our Savior & Lord, without the Holy Spirit, our nature, doing life without transformation, is every man, woman, and child, doing what is right in their own eyes (their own opinion): *What I want!* The Book of Judges shows us, tells us, what mankind is like when there is no restraint on them (no king in Israel). Chapters 17 through 21 portray multiple examples.

> The heart is the most deceitful thing there is and desperately wicked. No one can really know how bad it is! Only the Lord knows! He searches all hearts and examines deepest motives so he can give to each person his right reward, according to his deeds—how he has lived.
>
> -Jeremiah 17:9-10

Forgiveness and mercy do not come naturally to the human nature. Rebellion does. Comparing ourselves amongst ourselves does. Thinking of ourselves more highly than we should or thinking of ourselves as "not as good" does. Blame and babbling do.

NOTE: For example, when a drunk human drives and hurts or kills someone, they may say, "Not my fault. I was drunk and did not know what I was doing." Shifting the blame as Adam did when he told God, "but it was the woman you gave me … " (*see* Genesis 3:12).

So, again, the Bible tells us we become what we believe … what is in our hearts. Rooted and planted in our hearts … the most vital organ in the human body.

Chapter 3
Revelation Reveals Jesus

satan and his band of evil demons have also been around since before the day of our birth. Permissible by God, they have access to our lives and they are very good at what they do; touching circumstances, feeding our minds with deceptions and lies that lead us blindly down the path of despair and defeat … death while our hearts are pumping. They are mighty and strong. They are better at this spiritual battle than the human race is. They have much invested. They have much at stake. Envy and the desire to win drive them at all times. They do not ever "cease-fire." There is no sleep required and they feed from negative energy. We cannot fight them with our own energy, our own human strength. Coming to the end of self and all its negative impact, then raising our white flags to the Lord, is the wiser choice. Not the easier path. The wiser of the two choices. Surrendering to satan, or surrendering to the Creator, Adonai, Yeshua, the Holy Spirit, God, Love, the Scriptural way of life. Trusting God, to whom we cannot see with our physical eyes, does not come naturally. It is a learned behavior. Not "the easy" or "the convenient" road. Hearing His still small voice is an acquired talent that takes practice and meditation. However, the skill can be developed. And, to the power, to the level, each human so chooses.

> "I call heaven and earth to witness against you that today I have set before you life or death, blessing or curse. Oh, that you would choose life; that you and your children might live! Choose to love the Lord your God

and to obey him and to cling to him, for he is your life and the length of your days. You will then be able to live safely in the land the Lord promised your ancestors, Abraham, Isaac, and Jacob."

-Deuteronomy 30:19-20

In the Bible, God even gives us the answer. Dead-man dying? Or, dead-man living? We must understand though. Blindly living this life without understanding is like building a fighter jet with no training! These spiritual beings are real. Choosing to disregard them does not make them go away. If we feel we are not being affected by them, that my friend, is a dangerous path of travel. Coming to the end of self, self-indulgence, selfishness, is a process. Not a one-time decision. A process, like any other process, takes time and determination. It is individually learned. Pick a side and pursue it. We cannot serve two masters. Miserable Christians do not disciples make. We either believe in joy or we don't! We either commit to God or we don't!

Surveys say 75-80% of our US population "believe" in God. So, where is the evidence? Why is there a decaying value in Biblical values? Is it that "Christianity" has become just a title? Is it that we inherited the "I believe in God and go to church every Sunday" concept from our parents and grandparents, and therefore I have always been a Christian stance? If true Christianity is an internal conviction of sin and self, repentance of that [sin and self], which includes confession of that, then a turning away from all that [sin and self] plus surrendering to God, which it is, it cannot be solely a title or an idea. It is, it will be, an experience that changes one's life. It is asking our Creator to come into our lives, and, through His Spirit, help us run our lives. Then, keeping Him first in all of our decisions and actions, getting to know Him through His Word. Knowing of

Him does not a Christian make. Our parents and our titles do not get us into heaven; only Jesus does! Growing in Christ, absolutely, without a doubt, results in joy! Abundant life! The other side of happiness. The joy of the Lord is strength!

THIS IS FACT: God will not force any human being, who is mind, soul, and spirit, into putting Him first; EVER! He is quite the gentleman, and He invites whosoever!

> That is why I am suffering here in jail, and I am certainly not ashamed of it, for I know the one in whom I trust, and I am sure that he is able to safely guard all that I have given him until the day of his return.
>
> -2 Timothy 1:12

This is Paul speaking. A Pharisee among Pharisees. A killer of Christians. A writer of over one-third of the New Testament who was convicted, repented, and confessed, then turned from evil to God, saying to us, keep what you commit, regardless of circumstances (without bad, we cannot recognize good). When we are uncommitted, we have no desire for that relationship. No commit, no keep! Again, God does not force. He created humans, not robots. We have to, we must, choose! And then once the commitment, the follow through. Not stopping when we get off track. The Holy Spirit lets us know through intuition, an unction, and conviction, when we are off track. That is when we should say thank you, Heavenly Father, brush ourselves off, and keep pressing forward. All living sacrifices keep crawling off the altar. It is the Holy Spirit that supernaturally empowers us to endure and pursue the right relationship with God. An intimate, individual, relationship that we chose to commit to. However, this relationship, this supernatural, this spiritual relationship, requires coming to the end of "me, me, me, me, me, me, me", submission to the Father, and keeping God first in all things.

Always, daily, in the process of progress; not perfection! God only is perfection and He has a perfect plan for our lives. Indulgence of the flesh will not get us there.

> All of us used to be just as they are, our lives expressing the evil within us, doing every wicked thing that our passions or our evil thoughts might lead us into. We started out bad, being born with evil natures, and were under God's anger just like everyone else.
>
> -Ephesians 2:3

We were, by nature, children of wrath. Accepting this truth (the old human nature, the old man) and living life that way is death. And blaming it on somebody else is even worse. We have control over 'me'. Usually, when my life is not going in the direction it should, it is my fault and I can change it by turning to the Heavenly Father who loves me and gave His Son for me. Resisting evil is required! Verbally. Mentally. Daily. Constantly. Again, satan and his army of evil demons are very good at what they do—trickery, doubt, temptations. We, at our core, are an absolute mess without the Holy Spirit and Biblical wisdom. Every person is born a sinner and that sinful nature makes it easy to sin. Just as a dog has a dog nature, a human has a human nature—a sinful nature, fulfilling the desires of the flesh; going about life based on what we think. Remember, the battlefield is in the mind, trusting in self. It is not sins that make us sinners. And, God is not angry at sinners. He is angry at the sin. Praise God for His mercy and grace and the opportunity for reconciliation.

> When Adam sinned, sin entered the entire human race. His sin spread death throughout all the world, so everything began to grow old and die, for all sinned. We know that it was Adam's sin that caused this because although, of course, people were sinning from the time of Adam until Moses, God did not in those days

judge them guilty of death for breaking his laws—because he had not yet given his laws to them, nor told them what he wanted them to do. So when their bodies died it was not for their own sins since they themselves had never disobeyed God's special law against eating the forbidden fruit, as Adam had.

What a contrast between Adam and Christ who was yet to come! And what a difference between man's sin and God's forgiveness!

For this one man, Adam, brought death to many through his *sin*. But this one man, Jesus Christ, brought forgiveness to many through God's *mercy*. Adam's *one* sin brought the penalty of death to many, while Christ freely takes away *many* sins, and gives glorious life instead. The sin of this one man, Adam, caused *death to be king over all*, but all who will take God's gift of forgiveness and acquittal are *kings of life* because of this one man, Jesus Christ. Yes, Adam's *sin* brought *punishment* to all, but Christ's *righteousness* makes men *right with God*, so that they can live. Adam caused many to be sinners because he *disobeyed* God, and Christ caused many to be made acceptable to God because he *obeyed*.

The Ten Commandments were given so that all could see the extent of their failure to obey God's laws. But the more we see our sinfulness, the more we see God's abounding grace forgiving us. Before, sin ruled over all men and brought them to death, but now God's kindness rules instead, giving us right standing with God and resulting in eternal life through Jesus Christ our Lord.

-Romans 5:12-21

Born sinners. When a dog, when a canine is born, it is born with its nature. They urinate where they want. They smell all about the places they want to stick their noses. We can train them in all sorts of ways, but leave them on their own and watch them be a dog. Cats are cats with cat natures. Alligators are alligators with alligator natures. Sin entered into the perfect, created world, through one human man. The wages of sin is death. But all, whosoever, will take God's gift of forgiveness and acquittal, given to us by the one man, Jesus Christ, are His heirs here [on this earth] and there [in heavenly places]; on the dot and in heaven.

> So now, since we have been made right in God's sight by faith in his promises, we can have real peace with him because of what Jesus Christ our Lord has done for us. For because of our faith, he has brought us into this place of highest privilege where we now stand, and we confidently and joyfully look forward to actually becoming all that God has had in mind for us to be.
>
> -Romans 5:1-2

Not traditions and rituals. Not because of family or titles. Not because of words we speak. Yes, we most certainly need laws. Otherwise, where is the line? Without restrictions, we are left on our own; making up the rules as we go, basing them all on what we think!

> As he was starting out on a trip, a man came running to him and knelt down and asked, "Good Teacher, what must I do to get to heaven?"
>
> "Why do you call me good?" Jesus asked. "Only God is truly good! But as for your question—you know the commandments: don't kill, don't commit adultery, don't steal, don't lie, don't cheat, respect your father and mother."

"Teacher," the man replied, "I've never once broken a single one of those laws."

Jesus felt genuine love for this man as he looked at him. "You lack only one thing," he told him; "go and sell all you have and give the money to the poor—and you shall have treasure in heaven—and come, follow me."

Then the man's face fell, and he went sadly away, for he was very rich.

-Mark 10:17-22

Do you have "great possessions"? Jesus, the Good Teacher, is having a conversation with a rich, young ruler, a young man, with wealth and power. And, he, this man, left sorrowful since he was not willing to give it up. Should you continue reading Verses 23 through 31, we learn that less "self" is good. And, only God is perfect.

As the Scriptures say, "No one is good—no one in all the world is innocent."

-Romans 3:10

We cannot claim "goodness" on our own. Left on our own, we are sinners. The only way we can make ourselves feel good about ourselves is to compare ourselves [my this is better than your that; oh, I would never do what so-and-so did; listen to the way she or he talks, etc.] amongst ourselves.

Oh, don't worry, I wouldn't dare say that I am as wonderful as these other men who tell you how good they are! Their trouble is that they are only comparing themselves with each other, and measuring them-selves against their own little ideas. What stupidity!

-2 Corinthians 10:12

Thanking God that one is better than so-and-so is stupidity and certainly not an attribute of an intimate relationship with the Lord. God, in His mercy, forgives sinners. And sin is sin. Adultery to overeating. Religious, self-righteous people were rebuked by Jesus. Not the prostitutes, but the people who were proclaiming their own goodness. Jesus did not come to make up our deficits. Obedience is obedience. Disobedience is disobedience. Rebellion is rebellion. Without Jesus, left on our own, we are nothing but sinners.

> What are you so puffed up about? What do you have that God hasn't given you? And if all you have is from God, why act as though you are so great, and as though you have accomplished something on your own?
> -1 Corinthians 4:7

If that rubs us the wrong way, we are not submitted! Any good thing inside of us came from God! A gift given by God! All talents. All abilities. We are capable of developing them. But we played no part in the assignment of them.

Also, mature Christians must keep in mind, when a whosoever is converted to Christ, they do not, at that very moment, become nice. And, they most certainly will not instantly become like us! Impeccable manners and suitable Christian morals are learned. It is a process. It takes time, deter-mination, and commitment to the understanding of God's Word. Just as God is merciful to us, we are to be merciful to others. Bringing the Good News to people, planting the Seed of God is our goal. However, those humans have reputations, personalities, problems, and set mindsets; just like we did, just like we do! Hence, our journey in this life must be navigated through our own, individual, intimate relationship with God, our Creator! The Giver of the gifts and talents and abilities that one possesses plus is responsible for developing. The Holy Spirit helps us with this goodness. This holiness. This right-eousness. To initially be a little scared, a tiny bit unsure, or hesitant to trust Him is okay … maybe even a little bit normal. But the more we get into God's Word and get to know Him, the closer we can get to Him and the Holy Spirit; through the Holy Spirit. Walking, talking, trusting—these are parts of the process! It is a relationship! Relationships grow, dissolve, or remain one-sided when the primary focus remains self (me, myself, and I).

> But those enduring to the end shall be saved.
> -Matthew 24:13

Soon. 'Soon' will and does mean different things, certainly different times to the human race. Some of us may soon lose someone we love and their soon is for sure sooner than our soon. Some of us may be taken from here by way of evil forces, evil humans, death by violence. Some of us may die in an automobile accident. Some of us may have a good forty years or so left and depending on your age at this moment, forty years may or may not "seem" soon. However, endurance during that time period is critical. Whether we are or are *not* living in the world of the end, Jesus Christ will return. In our current culture, as with culture after culture after culture past, it is "easy" or it may "feel" easier to give up, throw in the towel; suicidal emotions are running rampant for a reason! But those who give up will not be able to embrace and enjoy the 'full' promised reward from the Lord God Almighty.

> "So stay awake and be prepared, for you do not know the date or moment of my return.["]
> -Matthew 25:13

Chapter 4
Two Choices

These momentary troubles on this little bitty planet in this big ole universe will be far outweighed by the promises of God for those who persevere. The end of age is soon, nearer, closer in time than when our Survival Guide was originally written. And yes, no one knows the date ... however, those who choose to remain faithful, even though there is a cultural assault going on, will be rewarded and continue eternal life with the Father, or, separated from the Father. This should be extremely exciting to us! Good News! It is a choice between two choices! Our Heavenly Father gave us the Blueprint ... full of prophecies ... warnings of deceptions ... warnings of famines and earthquakes becoming more frequent. He tells us of lawless-ness and lovelessness. He even says that many, multitudes of the human race who claim the title of "Christians" will fall away, give up on His Word ... their word. However, and once again, the positives outweigh the negatives. Once our sinful life has been wiped off the books, when we actively and purposefully grow in Christ plus endure, no day will pass, no grass will grow under our feet, as we mature in our experience of our Master, Savior, Jesus! So, of our own "soons", let's not lose a minute in building on what we have been given ... BY the Creator! Christians, true disciples of Christ, are to keep going during tough times ... to lock our feet in place and not move until Christ removes the load of this fallen world.

Jesus said, "No procrastination. No backward looks. You can't put God's kingdom off till tomorrow. Seize the day."

-Luke 9:62 MSG

Share in suffering as a good soldier of Christ Jesus. No soldier gets entangled in civilian pursuits, since his aim is to please the one who enlisted him.

2 Timothy 2:3-4 ESV

Many may stand and see, with our own physical eyes, the values of our USA, this whole world, all the nations, being decimated ... defying logic. Christians should be praying about this epidemic of the hatred of Truth and our integrity crisis daily. There are crazy beliefs left and right plus in the middle and all around our dot in the universe! Are you dead to sin? Have you turned to Christ? In title or totally? Where do you stand? Are we afraid of death ... when the heart, when that vital organ stops beating? Or, are we in the process, not wasting any time, serving God? Getting to know God. Allowing God to change us from the inside out ... until we stop breathing and we are spiritually lifted from this dot into the heavens. Spending time in the Living Word of God cleanses us, strengthens us, prospers us. Every time we hear the Word, when we allow it, it has a bearing on our lives. Whether student, lawyer, doctor, parent, or pastor ... whatever you are, whosoever you are ... God's Word will touch your life. There is that something about spending time with God that prospers our way.

> Oh, the joys of those who do not follow evil men's advice, who do not hang around with sinners, scoffing at the things of God: But they delight in doing everything God wants them to, and day and night are always meditating on his laws and thinking about ways to follow him more closely.
>
> They are like trees along a riverbank bearing luscious fruit each season without fail. Their leaves shall never wither, and all they do shall prosper.

But for sinners, what a different story! They blow away like chaff before the wind.   They are not safe on Judgment Day; they shall not stand among the godly.

For the Lord watches over all the plans and paths of godly men, but the paths of the godless lead to doom.

-Psalm 1

Those of us who meditate on God's Word, his leaves will not wither ... they will remain green. The Bible says "as thy days." The signs of this world tell us the older we are, the more days that are behind us, the more we decay. And, what happens, when we are not spending time with God, with the Holy Spirit, in God's Word, we begin to believe that. We expose ourselves to that decay and lose touch with what the Word of God says ... the flavor, the sweet aroma, the substance of God's Word. We are listening to the bad news on the news, basking in the stench of evil and evil-doers, watering bad seeds that are deeply rooted in our hearts versus what the Word says about us. People who are disconnected from God say what they say based on their upbringing, the experience they have had in and of this world, their five senses. The cleansing of the mind and the favor of God strengthens us so that we don't accept the things of this world so easily. So gullibly. Let those of us who have ears hear! Yahweh is always supernaturally working behind the scenes. The Word of God is a Book of Healing. A Book of Treasures. A Survival Guide for the victorious. When we touch God's Word and allow God's Word to touch us, we will come alive!   It is Living Water.   Living Water that is supposed to leak from our pores! Flow from our heart!

On the last day of the feast, the great day, Jesus stood up and cried out, "If anyone thirsts, let him come to me and drink. Whoever believes in me, as the Scripture has said, 'Out of his heart will flow rivers of living water.'"

✝

Now this he said about the Spirit, whom those who believed in him were to receive, for as yet the Spirit had not been given, because Jesus was not yet glorified.

-John 7:37-39 ESV

Jesus is risen! Now glorified! Come and thirst no more!

Chapter 5
Spiritual Maturity Brings The Word Alive in Our Hearts

We can either remain immature, a baby, in our Christian walk, and never experience the abundant life Jesus died to give us, or, we can choose to grow and mature for that abundant life here, on this earth.

> So get rid of your feelings of hatred. Don't just pretend to be good! Be done with dishonesty and jealousy and talking about others behind their backs. Now that you realize how kind the Lord has been to you, put away all evil, deception, envy, and fraud. Long to grow up into the fullness of your salvation; cry for this as a baby cries for his milk.
>
> -1 Peter 2:1-3

Many people believe they are to get born-again, then just hang around and wait to go to heaven. However, God has made provision for each of us. His will is that we grow up and enjoy what He has provided (this done deal).

Ephesians, Chapter 4, Verse 13 tells us to become more like Jesus as we walk through this world. Fully alive like Christ! When God asks that we do something, He gives us the power and the grace to do it. Our biggest mistake is to try [strive with our own might] and do it without the Helper [the Holy Spirit].

Our faith cannot grow without knowledge of Truth. More and more knowledge equals more and more and more faith. Only the Truth we know and act on will set us free. Freedom comes after we give up depending on "self" and instead, rely solely on God. *Growth in God.* Growing from baby's milk to solid food:

> You have been Christians a long time now, and you ought to be teaching others, but instead you have dropped back to the place where you need someone to teach you all over again the very first principles in God's Word. You are like babies who can drink only milk, not old enough for solid food. And when a person is still living on milk it shows he isn't very far along in the Christian life, and doesn't know much about the difference between right and wrong. He is still a baby-Christian!
>
> -Hebrews 5:12-13

To mature, we must become a living sacrifice, submitting to the will of God for our life. God's love for us should drive us, not the other way around. His plans for us are way better than our plans for ourselves. Romans, Chapter 12, Verses 1-2 tells us exactly what to do. *Then* He will give us the desires of our hearts. He will position the correct, true, fulfilling ones there; replacing the ones we "think" we want. Backsliding tends to keep us from His perfect will for our lives, or at least tremendously slow down the process. This should give us comfort!

> [F]or it was through reading the Scripture that I came to realize that I could never find God's favor by trying—and failing—to obey the laws. I came to realize that acceptance with God comes by believing in Christ.
>
> I have been crucified with Christ: and I myself no longer live, but Christ lives in me. And the real life I now have within this body is a result of my trusting in the Son of God, who loved me and gave himself for me.
>
> -Galatians 2:19-20

Jesus is on top of any problem we face. We are our own worst enemy. satan cannot use us without our consent and cooperation. Thinking in line with his deceptions will make us fall prey to his devouring. To treat those symptoms, we have to go through the process in His Word, holding tight to our faith in Christ, and it is personal! What am I meditating on? satan will do whatever he can to divert our attention from God. Whose approval do I seek? God's! It cannot be 'all about me and what I want.' God must be our Source and our life has to be spent learning the process of how to be totally dependent on Him. Submission to the Christ-follower lifestyle [intimate relationship with Christ] is key for spiritual maturity and life abundant. Eating of His Flesh and drinking of His Blood (*see* John 6:53-58).

To mature, there must be transformation, in the mind, from the old nature's way of thinking (*see* Romans 12:2). Otherwise, we will never experience the fullness of life in the way God has planned and purposed for us. If we don't actually know Absolute Truth, down in our hearts, it is dangerous. satan can prey upon our willingness to serve Christ wholeheartedly. Especially when we pick and choose the Verses of Scripture we like or think we know! It opens us up to trials and tribulations unprepared. So, again, if we are not getting to know God by way of our Survival Guide, our old nature will remain intact, our thinking will not change, and we cannot transform into the new creatures that we are [in Christ]. God will still love us, unconditionally, but, we will not be in the process of learning to love Him more. When we make the one-time decision to become a living sacrifice, like we are told to do in Romans 12:1, and do not metamorphose our old way of thinking into God's way of thinking, we are sitting ducks for satan and deception and ridicule and doubt and unfaith-fulness. Not to mention, we "react" based on our familiar [the roots of our individual pasts; history; what we have been taught; our individual experiences thus far], instead of settling into our new nature, like old leather.

Jesus' Parable of the Sower in Matthew 13, Mark 4, and Luke 8:4-15, tells us the importance of renewing the mind. It is THE TRUTH that sets us free, and only THE TRUTH that we know and sacrifice to do! It is the soil, the condition of our hearts, that make the Seeds grow—the Words, the Truth, from God. This, just like a tree in good soil, happens automatically [with the proper nourishment], just the way God created it to happen in Genesis 1:11-12. Consistent renewal of the mind comes automatically [when properly nourished], which changes us, from the nourished inside out [automatically], since the Word of God is the Incorruptible Seed (*see* 1 Peter 1:23), when it is rooted in good-heart! Good, rich, righteous heart, brings forth fruit. No fruit, no root. A seed activated in the nutrient rich soil and brings forth good fruit! "Let the earth bring forth ... grass, plants, trees ... " It is the soil that God made miraculous; the heart is miraculous. The heart brings forth fruit of itself. At the immediate instant of rebirth into the Christian lifestyle, our spirit is anew plus sealed by the Spirit of God. It is safe. It is secure. Your name is written in The Book of Life. We are no longer ungodly in our spirit. However, our old nature, our old opinions [what we want to believe], our old way of thinking, our bad habits, our addictions, our emotions, our flesh, our familiarities, like new leather, must be trans-formed. This is done by renewing the mind. Filling it with Truth. Rooting Truth in the good soil produces a godly life. The renewal of the mind is yet another key for spiritual maturity. To mature, we must utilize the Holy Spirit. This is where our discernment originates. The Holy Spirit is the One who wrote [inspired] the Word to our hearts, not to our human intellect. It is personal and it is intimate. This is how the Word of God comes alive in us (*see* John 16:13 and John 14:26). The job of the Holy Spirit is to reveal, disclose, the Bible to our hearts, *not* heads. It is alive, more powerful than the two-edged sword (*see* Hebrews 4:12). It pierces and divides the soul and spirit, exposing who we really are. Without the Holy Spirit, we cannot discern spiritual things, we are void of understanding. 1 Corinthians, Chapter 2, Verse 14 confirms this Truth.

Every single solitary time we are in a pit, the accuser of the brethren shows up and the condemnation begins. Without the assistance of the Holy Spirit, WHO NEVER, NEVER, NEVER condemns, His comfort and guidance and understanding cannot come. This is another huge reason why our minds must be renewed with Truth. Dealing with our thoughts, intellectually, daily, minute by minute, is inevitable! Since we cannot just turn the brain off and still function, we must allow the influence of the Holy Spirit to guide our thinking. The Holy Spirit inside of us produces the revelations, the unction, the "natural man" unknowing. Luke 24:32 describes this discern-ment and how it comes alive within us. The Bible, written through Holy Spirit relationship, must come alive in us so we can mature and experience the fullness of God, the Creator of all things (connection!).

> And I can't quit! For if I say I will never again mention the Lord—never more speak in his name—then his word in my heart is like fire that burns in my bones, and I can't hold it in any longer.
>
> -Jeremiah 20:9

ALIVE! Down in the most inner being of ourselves. Trans-forming our lives. When the Holy Spirit comes alive in us, our lives are transformed. The ministry of the Holy Spirit undeniably changes one's life if / when we stay consistently connected. There is not one human being on this planet who is too far away from their miracle. The more we respond in obedience to the quickening, unction, and revelation from the Holy Spirit, the sooner we will experience our breakthrough. Like the breath we breathe, we must stay connected morning, noon, and night, in order to remain spiritually alive and delight ourselves in the Lord, coming to the end of ourselves, out of the darkness, into the light. Otherwise, the world can suck the life, the Truth, the breath, right out of us! God wants to show Himself to each and every man, woman, and child on this earth. That is the Truth. The questions we must ask ourselves are: Do I want to know Him? To mature, to grow up, to experience the fullness and abundance and victory Jesus died for? It is necessary to depend on the revelation knowledge, the ministry, of the Spirit of the Holy One who lives on the inside of each and every, born-again Christian—just as Jesus told us! And, when we listen, we can feel and know the Spirit of the Lord moving and speaking just as plain and clear as Adam and Eve heard God, the sound of God, strolling in the Garden, in the evening breeze, in our hearts, through His Word, transforming our lives and our way of thinking!

To mature, we should utilize the power Jesus speaks of in Acts 1:8, " ... to testify about me with great effect ... " This resurrection power. Mark 16:20 tells us how this wonder-working power confirms the Word of God by the miracles, the moving of mountains, available through the Holy Spirit to those of us who live the Message; the disciples who allow the Word of God to come alive inside. It's like a well, full with fresh, clean drinking water. By faith, this well will not go dry. Jesus tells us in Mark 11:22-24, that if we believe, we have. And, just like a well, we must draw from it to benefit from it; when we only lean up against a well, we can die of thirst. Living Water has to be drawn from through the Holy Spirit. Learning how is another process that takes time, commitment, faith, understanding, praying in the Spirit, knowing God, being able to discern God's voice from the "ideas" that pop into the brain.

Prior to us ever showing up on planet earth, God made the decision that those who came to Him would be molded into the image of Jesus Christ. This means He is not going to just leave us alone to run around doing what we want to do whenever and wherever we want to do it! That is *not* love!

> For from the very beginning God decided that those who came to him—and all along he knew who would— should become like his Son, so that his Son would be the First, with many brothers.
> -Romans 8:29

Change glorifies God! An angry person who changes [transforms] into a person with a positive attitude and an open mind pleases God. If one used to be stingy, and now will literally give another their shirt from their back, this person is a little more like Yeshua, and God is pleased. If we just go to church because we feel like we have to in order to keep God happy, we are not only wrong, it sucks the joy from going to church from one's soul. Doing something, we believe to be "spiritual", like making yourself "read the Bible for two hours every day" with impure motives will become "law" to us. Creating a "have to" concept eventually leading to frustration and quitting. Besides, reading the Bible for two hours out of a commitment to the law does not an intimate relationship make! Sitting in a garage for two hours does not make you a car, right?

> You shouldn't have any trouble understanding this, friends, for you know all the ins and outs of the law— how it works and how its power touches only the living.

For instance, a wife is legally tied to her husband while he lives, but if he dies, she's free. If she lives with another man while her husband is living, she's obviously an adulteress. But if he dies, she is quite free to marry another man in good conscience, with no one's disapproval.

-Romans 7:1-3 MSG

Once again, let's ask ourselves: Am I the same person I was when I came to or returned to Christ? What changes have I made that now represent God well? Here is a fact to ponder: Any person who will not let God do what He wants to do in their life, will not ever be truly happy. You may limp along and have some kind of a life, and, praise God, you may even go to heaven, but you will be an unhappy Christian while you are here on this dot. It is like trying to put a square peg into a round hole. Ask: Do I spend my week waiting on Sunday, or do I enjoy my week with my Heavenly Father? Feeding my spirit? His Word is health to our mind and body.

For his Holy Spirit speaks to us deep in our hearts, and tells us that we really are God's children.

-Romans 8:16

Spiritual growth happens with the application of Truth, not simply knowing about Truth or knowing *about* God. There is no drive-through to spiritual maturity. It is a process that takes time and commitment and diligence. Christians who truly desire to mature as we are instructed in the Bible must get comfortable leaving the "milk" stage, embracing it, but growing beyond it. We should all want to be learning at all times to become skilled at righteousness. We must first know who we are in Christ; He has come to live in us at the new birth. My identity is now who I am in Him. This is where my confidence comes from. It is where my trust lies. Then, we begin to work with the Holy Spirit to let what He has done in us work to the outside of us so others recognize the change and desire to experience the peace, joy, and love they see. This changing, this transformation, requires correction (*not* condemnation) from God, meat from the Word of God, and much pruning.

> So there is now no condemnation awaiting those who belong to Christ Jesus.
>
> -Romans 8:1

When we know who we are in Christ, and when we allow the Holy Spirit to take the lead, we can take comfort in the fact that He is never going to show us something or deal with us about something if it is not the right time in our life and if it is not going to be for our benefit.

The Word of God is living and active, piercing to the division of soul and of spirit, of joints and of marrow, discerning the thoughts and intentions of the heart. When the promises of God are mixed with faith, His Word comes alive! God is with us 24 hours a day! *How much time do I spend with Him!*

> God means what he says. What he says goes. His powerful Word is sharp as a surgeon's scalpel, cutting through everything, whether doubt or defense, laying us open to listen and obey. Nothing and no one can resist God's Word. We can't get away from it—no matter what.
>
> -Hebrews 4:12-13 MSG

Chapter 6
Determination

We must identify our own distractions. In this moment in time, what matters most is our relationship with God. Connection with God, through the Spirit and the Word He has for each of us, is what truly matters. Whosoever can accept His invitation. This world is broken. Human nature fell because of one man. The Source for change is God. "But he who endures to the end will be saved," Matthew 24:13 AMPC. The end, the soon, is widely debated yet quite simple. People have all kinds of beliefs. Allow them to believe what they want. Christians shall not be moved. We are to stand strong until the rapture or death. We are called to be faithful. We are to pursue the Lord's will. Fight the good fight. Finish the race like we are told in 2 Timothy 4:7. Stamina. Do not waver.

> "But there is another urgency before me now. I feel compelled to go to Jerusalem. I'm completely in the dark about what will happen when I get there. I do know that it won't be any picnic, for the Holy Spirit has let me know repeatedly and clearly that there are hard times and imprisonment ahead. But that matters little. What matters most to me is to finish what God started: the job the Master Jesus gave me of letting everyone I meet know all about this incredibly extravagant generosity of God.["]
>
> -Acts 20:22-24 MSG

" ... this incredibly extravagant generosity of God." For who-soever. Our ministry is to testify to the gospel of the grace of

God. None of this world's distractions should be allowed to derail us because we are locked into the will of God for our lives! Because of what Jesus Christ did for us. Pick what you believe. Know what you believe. Become a student to know more. In the midst of cultural assault, know what you know, and become strong in the Lord. The enemy is here to kill, steal, and destroy, plus move us away from God and the positive influence we are to have on others. The word *he,* referenced in Matthew 24:13, is singular. It is personal. It is you. It is me. A personal intimate relationship with God is required.

The term salvation has more facets than the most rare, most precious diamond. It appears more than 150 times in the Old and the New Testaments. In each setting, it can mean or refer to different things. For example:

> And Moses said to the people, "Fear not, stand firm, and see the salvation of the Lord, which he will work for you today. For the Egyptians whom you see today, you shall never see again.["]
>
> > -Exodus 14:13 ESV

Moses, leading the people of God through the Red Sea, speaks of salvation in terms of God handling a situation.

> ["]There is salvation in no one else! Under all heaven there is no other name for men to call upon to save them."
>
> > -Acts 4:12

Peter speaks of the One Door into heaven. All-in-all, salvation, when we allow it, means that Jesus Christ, when we are in Jesus Christ, the Savior of whosoever, and we stand there, live [here] there, endure there, Jesus will rescue us from evil and bring us safely into His Heavenly Kingdom. But in order to start the race, we must *first* decide to start the race. Then stay in it until the end. It is a day-by-day process. Trials and tribulations can actually become fuel for our faith in God. With guidance from the Holy Spirit, we can transform pain into power. Learn to help others through what we have learned. Learn to be better by the mistakes and failures from our past.

Jesus Himself spoke of trials and tribulations throughout His ministry. *Again, how can we recognize good if there is no bad to base it on?* No testing, no results. When things come against us, we must decide if we believe what the Word says ... if we believe what we say we believe. Or, do we jump off the cliff because someone else tells us to? There should be no "everybody else is doin' it" in our faith stand! *How are we handling the bumps and bruises life throws at us? Bitter or better? Lemon-faced or with love for others? Misery loves company or exposing the Fruit of The Spirit?* Our attitudes and service are to be befitting of the King of kings. We are disciples of Jesus and we have been commanded to make disciples of Jesus. To reflect His love. To radiate His kindness. To be joyful in times of trouble. Choosing to react godly in difficult circumstances, till the end, which very well may be soon.

Do we allow God to use us so we can be known as God's people? It is a decision only you, only I, can make. Circumstances do not make God who He is. They allow us to become who we are. Who we choose to become. God is for us. God is with us. God does not punish us for the sins His Son already paid for! satan, however, is real and smart. Reallocate funds from our police departments for political motives! Pastors preaching perversions! God will never violate one's free will. There is a cultural assault goin' on! We are in a spiritual battle! We are either part of the problem or play a part in the solution!

Love wins! Evil and evil-doers will be separated from God. Criminal killings are all hate crimes committed by haters. Accidents happen. This human body eventually shuts down. It is God who wakes us in the mornings so those of us who are still breathing, hearts still pumping, can complete His purpose in this not-over-yet, evil defeated battle. Without God, we are incapable of controlling our emotions, our instincts:

> But I need something *more*! For if I know the law but still can't keep it, and if the power of sin within me keeps sabotaging my best intentions, I obviously need help! I realize that I don't have what it takes. I can will it, but I can't *do* it. I decide to do good, but I don't *really* do it; I decide not to do bad, but then I do it anyway. My decisions, such as they are, don't result in actions. Something has gone wrong deep within me and gets the better of me every time.
>
> -Romans 7:17-20 MSG

Our independence from God is what gets the human race into so much trouble! In our "flesh", in our human nature, we are not "really awesome"! We are born [from our mother's womb] lost, separated from God. Many times "flesh", in the Bible, refers to the body and soul. Once we are born-again, born anew, choose to turn from sin and to the Savior, we are *spiritually* brand new [a new creature]! Same unrenewed mind. Same heart. Same body. Same thinking process. Same habits. Same reactions to things that upset us, push our buttons. Same clothes in the closet. Same spouse and/or children. Same job. Same financial situation. Same computer and/or cell phone, and the same ole apps that were on them that morning when the Lord allowed us to wake! Just as Paul writes:

I know I am rotten through and through so far as my old sinful nature is concerned. No matter which way I turn I can't make myself do right. I want to but I can't.
-Romans 7:18

So, praise God, if our life is in a mess, we have the capability to do something about it. Instead of us assigning fault, we can work with the Holy Spirit and do something about it, make changes, by allowing Him control as we follow the processes in our Survival Guide, given to us by God! Our mental, emotional, and physical state were corrupted by the fall [at birth]. Not as God had intended. But as man chose [one man, in the Garden]. Once we "choose" life with God; our future can become so bright we have to wear shades [abundant]!

Chapter 7
It Begins With The Way We Think of God

It always starts with our belief [the opinion within our hearts] about God! How seriously do we take Him? How seriously do we take the whole matter? Do we know we will go to heaven after death, or are we afraid to die?

> Only in that way could he deliver those who through fear of death have been living all their lives as slaves to constant dread.
>
> -Hebrews 2:15

" ... through fear of death" were all their lifetime subject to bondage [slaves to constant dread]! The resurrection of Jesus is a core value guaranteeing there is life after death. Without the crucifixion of Christ, there is no resurrection. Christ's deliberate sacrifice not only displays the full extent of His Love, but without the resurrection, our Christian faith would be in vain and our freedom would be impossible [Jesus Christ of Nazareth would be a great man who died on a cross].

Jesus is a well-known, well-documented man. The Son of Man, Son of God, spoke often of His upcoming death and resurrection; both predictions of His sacrifice and resurrection (for whosoever).

> From then on Jesus began to speak plainly to his disciples about going to Jerusalem, and what would happen to Him there—that He would suffer at the hands of the Jewish leaders, that he would be killed, and that three days later he would be raised to life again.
>
> -Matthew 16:21

As they were going down the mountain, Jesus commanded them not to tell anyone what they had seen until after he had risen from the dead.

-Matthew 17:9

One day while they were still in Galilee, Jesus told them, "I am going to be betrayed into the power of those who will kill me, and on the third day afterwards I will be brought back to life again." And the disciples' hearts were filled with sorrow and dread.

-Matthew 17:22-23

As Jesus was on the way to Jerusalem, he took the twelve disciples aside, and talked to them about what would happen to him when they arrived.

"I will be betrayed to the chief priests and other Jewish leaders, and they will condemn me to die. And they will hand me over to the Roman government, and I will be mocked and crucified, and the third day I will rise to life again."

-Matthew 20:17-19

["]But after I have been brought back to life again, I will go to Galilee and meet you there."

-Matthew 26:32

"All right," Jesus replied, "this is the miracle I will do for you: Destroy this sanctuary and in three days I will raise it up!"

-John 2:19

Had this not been the true story, His story would have not been of supernatural, extraordinary, significance. The horrific crucifixion with no rising was an all-to-often [normal] death during that period in time. So again, the significance and proof of the resurrection is how Jesus' story is like no other; surviving generation after generation. Our spirits will rise and exist throughout time.

For those who may be unsure of the "proof" of the resurrection, and in addition to the miraculous "rolling away of the stone from the grave entrance" facts, there were hundreds, if not thousands, who were eyewitnesses to this history. Jesus appeared to men and to women, to groups and to individuals. He appeared in a house and on a street. Some appearances were short, and some were stretched out over time!

> After that he was seen by more than five hundred Christian brothers at one time, most of whom are still alive, though some have died by now.
> -1 Corinthians 15:6

Some of those five hundred brothers [and more than likely wives, women, and children] were still alive as Paul spoke of the resurrection to these people in Corinth gathering ... and no one disputed it!

> During the forty days after his crucifixion he appeared to the apostles from time to time, actually alive, and proved to them in many ways that it was really he himself they were seeing. And on these occasions he talked to them about the Kingdom of God.
> -Acts 1:3

Look around at the present-day evidence of the resurrection—the Christian faith is everywhere! It is very possible, that even though Jewish Christians continued to observe the Sabbath, they also began to worship on Sunday in celebration of the Messiah (see Acts 20:7), which, in itself, was a huge deal in that day! Christian ordinances such as baptism and communion are celebrations that represent a relationship with the Lord and are partaken in all over the world. And, above all, we can look around, with our own eyes, we can see the lives that have been changed. There is living testimony upon past testimony that can be heard by our own ears from true believers who have experienced a life forever changed [transformed]. You see, our God can quite literally reverse any situation!

Historically, cultures rise and fall on truth and lies; light and darkness; good and evil. Just look around at the anxiety that abounds. One could deduce the world's suicide rate has dramatically increased in the passing years should they so choose to research a decay in love verses hate, contentment with oneself verses chaos within one's soul. This spiritual battle will come to an end at some point, we usually refer to it as "soon".

> And so I solemnly urge you before God and before Christ Jesus—who will some day judge the living and the dead when he appears to set up his kingdom—to preach the Word of God urgently at all times, whenever you get the chance, in season and out, when it is convenient and when it is not. Correct and rebuke your people when they need it, encourage them to do right, and all the time be feeding them patiently with God's Word.
>
> -2 Timothy 4:1-2

Christians should calm down and cheer up! We are to show others by our lives, the way we live at all times, the right, the godly way to live! Just because we have plenty to be upset about does not mean we have to be upset. Worry is some-thing we allow. Emotions can flare up and sink down but we do not have to ride the rollercoaster with 'em.

"I am leaving you with a gift—peace of mind and heart! And the peace I give isn't fragile like the peace the world gives. So don't be troubled or afraid.["]

-John 14:27

Jesus leaves us His peace and the Comforter. The peace is between us and God *not* us and people (which is our responsibility).

A relaxed attitude lengthens a man's life; jealousy rots it away.

-Proverbs 14:30

We must learn the processes in the Word to stop allowing ourselves to be upset (especially with our fellowman, which is the representation of our Christian walk / preach / way / responsibility). A calm and undisturbed mind and heart are the life and health of the body. Strife and upset rots the bones!

We should preach to the world at all times, and, when necessary, use words. Knowing and speaking and acting [patiently feeding the multitudes] on the Truth is the only thing that saves us from lies. Strongholds are the lies we believe deep down in the most inner parts of ourselves, therefore truths to us. We should always be aware of what we are thinking about. The Bible is inspired by God Himself. He simply used willing humans to write it down!

The whole Bible was given to us by inspiration from God and is useful to teach us what is true and to make us realize what is wrong in our lives; it straightens us out and helps us do what is right.

-2 Timothy 3:16

When you go back and research, you will find that the USA has been so successful because it was built on a Scriptural foun-dation, the Declaration of Independence, for example. The

Bible was written over a period of 1,400 years (the Old Testament by 300 B.C. at the latest, and the New Testament during the Third Council of Carthage, A.D. 397) by over 40 different willing people from various nations.[1] Billions and billions of copies have sold, a number that grows every single year. Of all the Bible manuscripts, they read almost exactly alike. Scholars spend their lives studying these early manuscripts and have confirmed that the Bible is 100% reliable in its *vox* (meaning) and 99.5% in its *verba* (words) from the original autographs. These manuscripts can be found in museums, libraries and churches around the world for anyone to explore.[2] Most were pen stroke differences (strokes that did not form a complete letter perfectly) and punctuation marks. The good news for us is that the scribal errors of spelling and inserted or omitted words are normally obvious and easy to spot. They take nothing away from the reliability of the original manuscripts or the basic message of the Bible.[3] The Word of God is absolute!

When people do not use the Bible as their foundation for truth, their truths constantly change based on what they believe to be true at that moment in time. Absolute Truth cannot change because then it ain't true! The Bible is Divine Truth:

> "What is truth?" Pilate exclaimed. Then he went out again to the people and told them, "He is not guilty of any crime.["]
>
> -John 18:38

[1] Willmington, H L. Willmington's Bible Handbook. Wheaton, Ill., Tyndale House Publishers, 1997.
[2] "A Case for the Bible 101: Manuscript Evidence Part 11 – Are There Errors in the Manuscripts?" Truth, Faith and Reason, 12 May 2018, truthfaithandreason.com/a-case-for-the-bible-101-manuscript-evidence-part-11-are-there-errors-in-the-manuscripts/.
[3] "How Reliable Are the Ancient Biblical Manuscripts in Our Possession? - Eternal Perspective Ministries." Eternal Perspective Ministries, 2024, www.epm.org/resources/2024/Jun/28/reliable-biblical-manuscripts/.

Jesus said to them, "You are truly my disciples if you live as I tell you to, and you will know the truth, and the truth will set you free."

-John 8:31-32

Once we become disciples of Christ and learn how to do what God wants us to do while our "flesh" is screaming at us not to do it, we will be free! If we are saying, doing, acting on anything that is *not* in agreement with the Scriptures, we must *learn* how to replace it with what is! The Bible tells us to take every thought captive [see it, seize it] and make it obedient to Jesus Christ. Do not conform to the pattern of this fallen world. Do not participate in the cultural assault. Do not be alarmed by this cultural assault. Be transformed by the renewal of the mind. If we are "too busy", we should be willing to adjust our schedule. If we are "too tired", exercise. If we are "too selfish", begin helping those who have less. The process involves peeling back the layers to get to the core of the stronghold.

Every human being starts life with an intuitive knowledge of right and wrong! Close your eyes for a moment and look back on something you did in younger times ... you knew that something was wrong [sin], yet did it anyway, and then got that "conviction" deep down inside, in the core of your being. That intuitive knowledge of right and wrong!

[A]nd how from childhood you have been acquainted with the sacred writings, which are able to make you wise for salvation through faith in Christ Jesus. All Scripture is breathed out by God and profitable for teaching, for reproof, for correction, and for training in righteousness, that the man of God may be complete, equipped for every good work.

-2 Timothy 3:15-17 ESV

When the human race was originally created, with free will, they had no formal education. There were no schools and colleges for celebrating one's degree or valedictorianship as our current culture so does. Some simply "chose" to follow good. Others "chose" bad and evil; some barbaric even! The uncivilized and savage man knows (or once knew) they are doing wrong and they should be treating others the way they would like to be treated; until they reach the point of reprobate! Once we become hard-hearted, we lose all sense of conviction. However, we did not start out that way!

The Bible, Jesus Christ, lets us know (in relation to speaking about Truth) to *act* on the Truth we know and God will give us more. Deny the Truth we know, and He will take, even the little bit we may know, away:

> ["]For to the one who has, more will be given, and he will have an abundance, but from the one who has not, even what he has will be taken away.["]
>
> -Matthew 13:12 ESV

Truth [Biblical Truth] comes through revelation. Embrace it! People who do what is right [act from God-breathed intuitiveness] but do not believe in the Bible are acting out of consciousness; God will eventually turn them over to a reprobate mind [seared conscience]. Just as satan used the tree of the knowledge of good and evil [Truth] in the Garden of Eden, he has to separate the people from the Scriptures to get [manipulate / trick] them into sin. The Truth that we do not know is how satan gains access to us. Without the learning comes the strongholds!

> Jesus told him, "I am the Way–yes, and the Truth and the Life. No one can get to the Father except by means of me."
>
> -John 14:6

Jesus is the Way. And not all who say, "Lord, Lord" are going to enter the Gates of Heaven. Matthew 24: 12 tells us, "Sin will be rampant everywhere and will cool the love of many," because many false prophets will appear and lead many astray. A false message is anything that deviates from the Word of God, ranging from information or opinions totally against the Bible, or more subtle manipulation of the Scriptures. We must be totally aware of what the Bible teaches, not vainly calling Him, 'Lord, Lord', without sub-mission to His ways! Here is the Good News: Whosoever truly repents and turns from evil (not just goes through the motions) can become a genuine disciple and enter the Gates, abundantly!

> For no prophecy recorded in Scripture was ever thought up by the prophet himself. It was the Holy Spirit within these godly men who gave them true messages from God.
>
> -2 Peter 1:20-21

> Every part of Scripture is God-breathed and useful one way or another—showing us truth, exposing our rebellion, correcting our mistakes, training us to live God's way.
>
> -2 Timothy 3:16 MSG

Peter gave this explanation of what he believed; he knew he was fixin' to die, and he witnessed with his eyes what he spoke:

> They have gone off the road and become lost like Balaam, the son of Beor, who fell in love with the money he could make by doing wrong; but Balaam was stopped from his mad course when his donkey spoke to him with a human voice, scolding and rebuking him.

These men are as useless as dried-up springs of water, promising much and delivering nothing; they are as unstable as clouds driven by the storm winds. They are doomed to the eternal pits of darkness. They proudly boast about their sins and conquests, and, using lust as their bait, they lure back into sin those who have just escaped from such wicked living.

-2 Peter 2:15-18

Unfortunately, too many Christians in this world, on this dot, the ones within the over 8 billion, would not STAND and defend that the Word of God is accurate. Somehow, more than likely the pressures from cultural assaults, people have gotten to where they believe the criticisms and choose not to put real faith and belief in the Word.

The Word of God is a supernatural book, there is no other like it. It is ABSOLUTE, and we can build our lives upon it.

We must develop a love for God's Word—a heart for God's Word. Those who claim they do not get anything out of it are those who are not doing anything with it. Either sin will keep you from the Bible or the Bible will keep you from sin!

Chapter 8
Christ-Followers Are New Creatures

So, again, as a man thinketh [within the most vital organ of his being], without the renewal of the mind, the thoughts will not change. Biblical views and values are in the Bible. Transformation comes from the inside out, not from the outside in. To see things clearly, we have to see God and who He is clearly. Through His Word. Jesus Christ as His Son and our Savior and our LORD. The Holy Spirit as a Friend. We are dead-to-sin [crucified with Christ at our second birth].

> So what do we do? Keep on sinning so God can keep on forgiving? I should hope not! If we've left the country where sin is sovereign, how can we still live in our old house there? Or didn't you realize we packed up and left there for good? That is what happened in baptism. When we went under the water, we left the old country of sin behind; when we came up out of the water, we entered into the new country of grace—a new life in a new land!

> That's what baptism into the life of Jesus means. When we are lowered into the water, it is like the burial of Jesus; when we are raised up out of the water, it is like the resurrection of Jesus. Each of us is raised into a light-filled world by our Father so that we can see where we're going in our new grace-sovereign country.

> Could it be any clearer? Our old way of life was nailed to the cross with Christ, a decisive end to that sin-miserable life—no longer captive to sin's demands! What we believe is this: If we get included in Christ's sin-conquering death, we also get included in his life-

saving resurrection. We know that when Jesus was raised from the dead it was a signal of the end of death-as-the-end. Never again will death have the last word. When Jesus died, he took sin down with him, but alive he brings God down to us. From now on, think of it this way: Sin speaks a dead language that means nothing to you; God speaks your mother tongue, and you hang on every word. You are dead to sin and alive to God. That's what Jesus did.

-Romans 6:1-11 MSG

Dead to sin! We are allowed to leave all the nasty, all the bad, all the guilt and condemnation, at the very bottom of the baptism pool! We are now cleansed of that sinful nature because of what Jesus did, for whosoever, on that cross!

However, we now have to cleanse our minds from where that draw, that tendency to act on and react from things we have become accustomed to from birth to the second we were saved. The entire time the old nature was in charge [this from-birth, mind-programming]. Anger. Bitterness. Resentment. Criticism. We cannot reject what the Word says just because we still observe our actions and thoughts and emotions which are/have been programmed how to be selfish, how to lust, how to be rebellious ... how to _be_ the old man [self-centered]. Like a computer program, we have to reprogram our brains, our minds. We must die to sin and sinful thoughts. Continuing to think wrong [the from-birth-programming] cannot bring us into the fullness of Christ.

Your old evil desires were nailed to the cross with him; that part of you that loves to sin was crushed and fatally wounded, so that your sin-loving body is no longer under sin's control, no longer needs to be a slave to sin;

-Romans 6:6

We have to know this in our hearts. We cannot know what we do not know. Spiritual growth, knowledge of HIM, must become a priority to all Christians. Growing in HIM day by day by day. We are to be useful. We are to be fruitful. We must make time to get to know Him. Relationship with Him to discover what He wants from us. For the benefit of HIS Kingdom. Heaven is a big deal. What are our visions? How are we coping with life's troubles? Do we sometimes feel hopelessness or despair?

Now, let's ask ourselves again: What is my vision?

> Since God has so generously let us in on what he is doing, we're not about to throw up our hands and walk off the job just because we run into occasional hard times. We refuse to wear masks and play games. We don't maneuver and manipulate behind the scenes. And we don't twist God's Word to suit ourselves. Rather, we keep everything we do and say out in the open, the whole truth on display, so that those who want to can see and judge for themselves in the presence of God.

> If our Message is obscure to anyone, it's not because we're holding back in any way. No, it's because these other people are looking or going the wrong way and refuse to give it serious attention. All they have eyes for is the fashionable god of darkness. They think he can give them what they want, and that they won't have to bother believing a Truth they can't see. They're stone-blind to the dayspring brightness of the Message that shines with Christ, who gives us the best picture of God we'll ever get.

Remember, our Message is not about ourselves; we're proclaiming Jesus Christ, the Master. All we are is messengers, errand runners from Jesus for you. It started when God said, "Light up the darkness!" and our lives filled up with light as we saw and understood God in the face of Christ, all bright and beautiful.

If you only look at us, you might well miss the brightness. We carry this precious Message around in the unadorned clay pots of our ordinary lives. That's to prevent anyone from confusing God's incomparable power with us. As it is, there's not much chance of that. You know for yourselves that we're not much to look at. We've been surrounded and battered by troubles, but we're not demoralized; we're not sure what to do, but we know that God knows what to do; we've been spiritually terrorized, but God hasn't left our side; we've been thrown down, but we haven't broken. What they did to Jesus, they do to us—trial and torture, mockery and murder; what Jesus did among them, he does in us—he lives! Our lives are at constant risk for Jesus' sake, which makes Jesus' life all the more evident in us. While we're going through the worst, you're getting in on the best!

We're not keeping this quiet, not on your life. Just like the psalmist who wrote, "I believed it, so I said it," we say what we believe. And what we believe is that the One who raised up the Master Jesus will just as certainly raise us up with you, alive. Every detail works to your advantage and to God's glory: more and more grace, more and more people, more and more praise!

So we're not giving up. How could we! Even though on the outside it often looks like things are falling apart on us, on the inside, where God is making new life, not a day goes by without his unfolding grace. These hard times are small potatoes compared to the coming good times, the lavish celebration prepared for us. There's far more here than meets the eye. The things we see now are here today, gone tomorrow. But the things we can't see now will last forever.

-2 Corinthians 4:1-18 MSG

"You" is the church [God's chosen. God's people. We, the Christian people.] in Paul's trial and torture teaching in 2 Corinthians, Chapter 4. Let's read it again, this time from The Living Bible translation:

It is God himself, in his mercy, who has given us this wonderful work of telling his Good News to others, and so we never give up. We do not try to trick people into believing—we are not interested in fooling anyone. We never try to get anyone to believe that the Bible teaches what it doesn't. All such shameful methods we forego. We stand in the presence of God as we speak and so we tell the truth, as all who know us will agree.

If the Good News we preach is hidden to anyone, it is hidden from the one who is on the road to eternal death. Satan, who is the god of this evil world, has made him blind, unable to see the glorious light of the Gospel that is shining upon him or to understand the amazing message we preach about the glory of Christ, who is God. We don't go around preaching about ourselves but about Christ Jesus as Lord. All we say of ourselves is that we are your slaves because of what Jesus has done for us. For God, who said, "Let there be light in the darkness," has made us understand that it is the brightness of his glory that is seen in the face of Jesus Christ.

But the precious treasure—this light and power that now shine within us—is held in a perishable container, that is, in our weak bodies. Everyone can see that the glorious power within must be from God and is not our own.

We are pressed on every side by troubles, but not crushed and broken. We are perplexed because we don't know why things happen as they do, but we don't give up and quit. We are hunted down, but God never abandons us. We get knocked down, but we get up again and keep going. These bodies of ours are constantly facing death, just as Jesus did; so it is clear to all that it is only the living Christ within who keeps us safe.

Yes, we live under constant danger to our lives because we serve the Lord, but this gives us constant opportunities to show forth the power of Jesus Christ within our dying bodies. Because of our preaching, we face death, but it has resulted in eternal life for you.

We boldly say what we believe trusting God to care for us, just as the psalm writer did when he said, "I believe and therefore I speak." We know that the same God who brought the Lord Jesus back from death will also bring us back to life again with Jesus and present us to him along with you. These sufferings of ours are for your benefit. And the more of you who are won to Christ, the more there are to thank him for his great kindness, and the more the Lord is glorified.

That is why we never give up. Though our bodies are dying, our inner strength in the Lord is growing every day. These troubles and sufferings of ours are, after all, quite small and won't last very long. Yet this short time of distress will result in God's richest blessing upon us forever and ever! So we do not look at what we can see right now, the troubles all around us, but we look forward to the joys in heaven which we have not yet seen. The troubles will soon be over, but the joys to come will last forever.

-2 Corinthians 4:1-18

If we have ever seen a fish that is still alive and removed from water, we see, with our physical eyes, how they flip and flop and twist and bend. The entire time they are in that fight-mode, they are contributing to their own demise ... quickening their own physical death while trying to make it ... trying to make it in an environment they are not created for.

The same holds true for humans. Men are not created to live in the water [spiritually: this fallen world]. However, if we take an oxygen tank into the water, a physical, breathing-while-under-the-water mechanism, into that place, that environment we are not created for, we can exist for a while.

When we accept Jesus Christ of Nazareth, Yeshua, as our personal Savior and Lord, we transfer out of the kingdom of darkness, into the Kingdom of Light, and we now have a tank, a breathing mechanism, that we are to wear in this fallen world. We can make it here, because we have access to heaven's world. Because of Jesus' sacrifice and resurrection, we have heaven's air! When heaven becomes a big deal to us, we can breathe better. We have the capability to cope! The Word of God is our breathing mechanism in this fallen, in this foreign world. Our life after death is in heaven. Trials and torture and troubles are traded for treasures there. God's richest blessings upon us forever and ever! Heaven is a BIG DEAL. This world, this dot, is real, but it is temporary.

Stop loving this evil world and all that it offers you, for when you love these things you show that you do not really love God; for all these worldly things, these evil desires—the craze for sex, the ambition to buy everything that appeals to you, and the pride that comes from wealth and importance—these are not from God. They are from this evil world itself. And this world is fading away, and these evil, forbidden things will go with it, but whoever keeps doing the will of God will live forever.

-1 John 2:15-17

This world, this physical world, this foreign land, is under satan's power and control. Therefore, if we are living for the physical, we are living for satan ... the physical pleasure of flesh, buying up everything we can accumulate ... things that appeal to us just because we want to have 'em ... and pride ... recognition, the pursuit to be significant, the desire to be known for our wealth and importance ... floppin' around like a fish outside of water. And, when we fall out of love with God and into love with the evil things, it will not go well. We risk forfeiting our place [our assignment] in heaven. We risk giving up the writing of our name in the Lamb's Book

God's children, God's chosen, authentic Christians, never give up. We choose to turn from sin. We choose not to react like that fish who is trying to make it in the wrong environment. We are in the process of improving on our spiritual eyesight. In Chapter 4 of 2 Corinthians, Paul identifies three ways for us to look at things differently. Guidance for getting off the road that leads to eternal death. Three different ways to work on our Christian lifestyle. How to prioritize our spiritual life while we exist in this physical world. How to remain in intimate, personal relationship with our Heavenly Father. This is why we were created! When we do life in relationship with God, there's gonna be struggles, but this world is temporary. Heaven is a big deal.

The Corinthian Christians who Paul was addressing were a rebellious people. Paul understood salvation, and he knew the relationship between God and the people. God and you. God and me. It is personal. It is an experience that is most important in one's life! Paul is telling us, if we can work on our eyesight [vision], we can change our hearts and our "fainting" [giving up] situation!

> That is why we never give up. Though our bodies are dying, our inner strength in the Lord is growing every day.
>
> -2 Corinthians 4:16

Our outside, our fleshly body, is aging. It is temporary. Our spirit man is eternal. Which man are we focusing on? Are we looking at the external us, or, is it important to us that our inner man, us on the inside, where God is, is being renewed? Getting spiritually renewed. Getting stronger. Spiritual endurance includes God. It builds Christlike character. There is not a day that goes by that we should not be prioritizing our inside self over the physical. To get old on the outside and on the inside brings on multiple problems in itself. Ones that can be avoided! Starving oneself, one's God-made self, causes drooping of the head ... dragging of the feet ... and sooner or later, regardless of our condition, we all have to face God [the Judgement Seat of Christ]. If we are going to cope with the confusion of this dot, if we are going to cope with difficulties, we must feed our spiritual man ... with Word, with prayer, with bringing God in on the decisions we make day in and day out. One Man died for every one of us. That puts every one of us in the same boat. We all have the same free will. My will or God's will be done. If things are falling apart on the outside, we must ask ourselves: "Am I lighting up the darkness?" The renewal of our minds is imperative! Paul says, if you are not going to lose heart [not give up] we must renew [resurrect] our inner man day-by-day. Grow in spirit, day after day after day. God says if we want to hang in there when the going gets tough, it is [it requires] a day-by-day renewal of the inner man. The from-birth, mind programming [way of thinking] must catch up with the "new creature" way of thinking. If this renewal is not taking place, our insides are dying just like our outsides. Again, free will, free choice. As the prophet Jeremiah spoke aloud unto the Lord:

> Your words are what sustain me; they are food to my hungry soul. They bring joy to my sorrowing heart and delight me. How proud I am to bear your name, O Lord.
>
> -Jeremiah 15:16

So again, we must ask ourselves: What did I spiritually eat today [Did I receive any Word inwardly into my soul ... like milk into the belly]? Am I quite content to physically die, because then, I will be at home with the Lord?

When we are born-again, God puts within us Himself. We get a brand-new Spirit that is identical to His Spirit:

> By this is love perfected with us, so that we may have confidence for the day of judgment, because as he is so also are we in this world.
>
> -1 John 4:17 ESV

The Bible promises God's disciples that God, on the inside of us, will keep those of us whose mind is stayed upon Him in perfect peace:

He will keep in perfect peace all those who trust in him,
whose thoughts turn often to the Lord!

-Isaiah 26:3

Please, stop everything you are doing right now. Close your
eyes and ask yourself: Am I at peace?

What was your vision? Did you see the Father? Did you see
your problem? Do you have a real desire to improve your
spiritual eyesight?

Notes:

_____
_____
_____
_____
_____
_____
_____
_____
_____
_____
_____
_____
_____
_____
_____
_____
_____
_____
_____
_____
_____

Chapter 9
What is My Focus?

There is a cultural assault goin' on. If we are going to cope with chaos, if we are going to cope with confusion, if we are going to cope with difficulties, day-by-day, day in and day out, we must feed [nourish] the spiritual man by spending quality time with God! We naturally operate on a daily mindset [every nanosecond of every day, our minds are in operation, making decisions, thinking on things, absorbing data, processing information]. This requires consistent spiritual nourishment of the inner man and the renewal of the mind to keep the spirit man healthy [nourished properly]. This gives the Holy Spirit, the God inside us, the daily bread necessary to thrive, to breathe in this foreign land, so our physical man can cope on a spiritual level and not become faint. So we will not lose heart.

The second thing Paul tells the church (Jesus' disciples who are equipped with their breathing mechanisms, lighting up the dark) in 2 Corinthians, Chapter 4 is:

> These troubles and sufferings of ours are, after all, quite small and won't last very long. Yet this short time of distress will result in God's richest blessing upon us forever and ever!
>
> -2 Corinthians 4:17

Paul is speaking spiritually. He is not saying our pains don't hurt. They do. We all experience them. The church and the ungodly. He is stating that our riches, our Christian treasures, are in Heaven. Down here, on this dot, in this fallen world, is momentary. These troubles are not measured against a clock. They are measured against eternity. This earth's timetable is temporary, and, focusing on that, not thinking outside the box, will mess us up on the inside! We live in the balance of grace and faith. God's grace. Our faith. Neither of those can be seen. Obedience strengthens us. Truth holds us in hard times. Because of Yeshua, we have access to heaven. Heaven is a big deal. That, my friend, should give you peace! These bodies are dying. Our spirits are not. What we can see right now is short. Resting in what Jesus has done for us ... this is peace, eternal. Entering into this kind of rest requires feeding our inner man on a daily basis, and not giving up!

Wanting more of what we have down here, which, by the way, is by the grace of God, not coincidence, not luck, will cause us to lose our way. To lose our focus. If somehow you are there right now, it is okay. God still loves you. All you gotta do is ask Him: "Lord, where have I wandered away from Your perspective?" As we study the life of Jesus, we will truly see that He consistently stayed connected [in sync] spiritually to the Father, and kept His eyes on His place in heaven.

Because of God, the Creator, because of Yeshua, the Savior, because of the Holy Spirit that lives within us, heaven is our home. And, when we get a clear view of that, we can see with new eyes! The blind can now see. Desperation becomes hope. Drama becomes sheer delight! Heaven, my friends, is a big deal. Eternity with the Father is a big deal. Remaining young and strong on the inside is a big deal. Inside this decaying, physical man, is a treasure chest! There is a lavish celebration prepared for us! When we look toward eternity, while we are functioning in time, with our breathing mechanism. Our Survival Guide. These hard times are small potatoes. God is making new life on the inside of us. If all we live for is now, now is all we get. Heaven helps us in our nows!

What are we looking at? Can we vision our new eyes? We are heirs to the KINGDOM, praise God! I am encouraging each one of us to begin the process of improving our eyesight! We can sleep better. We can stand stronger. We can look forward to our wonderful new bodies in heaven. Whatever is causing us to lose heart can change because we will be looking at it from God's perspective. God's point of view. However, we must decide what we want. It is not an obligation, and God will NEVER violate our free will. This commitment and change is a choice. Once we are saved, once we surrender, God is with us. God is in us. Now we can look forward, with confidence, to our heavenly bodies, realizing that every minute we spend in these decaying bodies, is time spent away from our time WITH GOD!

So, the third thing we want to discuss, and this is certainly not third in order of importance, is the opening statements of Verses 1 and 2. "WE", the Christians, the Christ followers who walk by faith and not by sight to ensure we are pleasing to our Father in heaven. The disciples who live from our hearts. We speak Truth, patiently and in love, from our mouths. Every day we are feeding our inner man. We live and walk with character. We hold Biblical standards, Biblical worldviews, Biblical values, highest priority. We know plus respect that God Himself, in His mercy, has given us this wonderful work, this precious privilege, of telling this Good News to others. Without giving up. Without throwing in the towel. Without flipping and flopping like a fish out of water.

It is God who has granted us favor. It is God who has made our salvation freely available, and therefore granting us access into heaven. Once we have turned from our shameful, sinful nature so that all who know us, and even the human beings who do not know us, are able to see the God within us. Our desire, our commitment, is to represent Him well, with excellence, everywhere we go. For we know and love that we stand, at all times, in the presence of God. Our lives are an open book of truth to others with no manipulations, no twisting of God's Word involved. This way, those who are of this world, can see Jesus in us. For some, we are the best picture of God they will ever see. Our eyes are improving every day. Heaven is a big deal to us. We understand that our decision to follow Christ is the single-most important decision we will ever make. A choice between life abundant and a meaningless existence. We understand that the daily feeding of our spirit man is of the utmost importance. The choice between life and death. We are hard-pressed on every side, but not crushed. We do not know why things happen as they do, but we don't give up and quit. We have been, and will continue to be, spiritually terrorized. But God's incomparable power within us keeps us strong, courageous, and careful. Our lifestyle reflects the resurrection of Jesus. Life is at work within us, plus we know the One who raised Him! We are in a daily, heart-to-heart, relationship with Him! Yes, we are in this world. However, we are drawing life, through our breathing mechanism, from our eternal environment. This is why we do not lose heart. For our light and momentary troubles are achieving for us an eternal glory that far outweighs them all!

If you are reading, if you are listening to these words, and if you are in any kind of emotional despair or a wilderness of addiction or if you feel like quitting or giving up … please, we are begging you, make a choice and stick with it. Get thee behind me despair and discouragement. As for me and my house, we are gonna serve the Lord!

The Gospel of John, Chapters 14, 15, and 16 are three wonderful teachings on relationship with the Holy Spirit. I am encouraging each of us to take the time to study them. Start today. Do not quit. Do not throw in the towel until every Word of John 14, 15, and 16 are deep inside! Fill your jars of clay with treasures from above. The spiritual internal is much more important than this physical external. Don't be a flopping fish. Use your breathing mechanism [your Survival Guide] PLEASE! DO NOT LEAVE GOD OUT!

Chapter 10
The Judgment Seat of Jesus

National Football League (NFL) players are evaluated on Mondays by the tape of their actions from Sunday's game. A position coach, the team official in charge of coaching a specific position group, analyzes each player from that particular position, going over and evaluating the good, the bad, and the ugly. Wonder the thoughts that would be in their minds … each player knowing they were fixin' to be judged based on their performance.

Now, let's think about this (although this scenario is on a totally different scale): Each and every man will stand before the Lord for an evaluation, and He is going to show us our tape. How was my performance as a Christian? How did I function as a Christian? Our evaluation will most certainly take place, and it will be a determination of the gain or loss of my rewards. Surely, we all know that our God is a jealous God:

> You shall not bow down yourself to them or serve them;
> for I the Lord your God am a jealous God …
> -Exodus 20:5 AMPC

> For the Lord your God is a consuming fire, a jealous God.
> -Deuteronomy 4:24 AMPC

We also know that Jesus paid a high price on that cross! Christ brought us, the church, together through His death on that cross. And God is building us a home in the heavens. We belong there and He is using the church in what He is building. The foundation of the church was laid by the apostles and the prophets:

> You are built upon the foundation of the apostles and prophets with Christ Jesus Himself the chief Cornerstone.
>
> -Ephesians 2:20 AMPC

... those who God authorized to write the Scriptures. We should all look to the Word of God as the architectural drawings for the buildings of our lives, and the Cornerstone of that building is Jesus Christ Himself. Without the Cornerstone, a building will lose its integrity! Jesus Christ must be the point of reference for all of life. We have to remain committed and focused on our foundation so that we can keep our parts together. We should see it taking shape day after day ... a holy temple built by God! God does not want our life to be built by someone who does not appreciate the price Jesus paid on the cross. First Timothy, Chapter 2, Verse 4, reads that God's desirable will is for all to be saved and to understand His Truth. He actually longs for this. However, He will not impose His desirable will upon our free will. Do we live in appreciation of the high price, the finished work, paid for us on that cross?

First Corinthians, Chapter 10, and Verse 31 reads, "... we must do everything for the glory of God ...". God wants to be involved in every area of our lives ... every element. Decisions, choices, directions, relationships, chores ... you name it! His involvement attaches eternal value.

> God, in his kindness, has taught me how to be an expert builder. I have laid the foundation and Apollos has built on it. But he who builds on the foundation must be very

careful. And no one can ever lay any other real foundation than that one we already have—Jesus Christ. But there are various kinds of material that can be used to build on that foundation. Some use gold and silver and jewels; and some build with sticks, and hay, or even straw! There is going to come a time of testing at Christ's Judgment Day to see what kind of material each builder has used. Everyone's work will be put through the fire so that all can see whether or not it keeps its value, and what was really accomplished. Then every workman who has built on the foundation with right materials, and whose work still stands, will get his pay. But if the house he has built burns up, he will have a great loss. He himself will be saved, but like a man escaping through a wall of flames.

Don't you realize that all of you together are the house of God, and that the Spirit of God lives among you in his house? If anyone defiles and spoils God's home, God will destroy him. For God's home is holy and clean, and you are that home.

Stop fooling yourselves. If you count yourself above average in intelligence, as judged by this world's standards, you had better put this all aside and be a fool rather than let it hold you back from the true wisdom from above. For the wisdom of this world is foolishness to God. As it says in the book of Job, God uses man's own brilliance to trap him; he stumbles over his own "wisdom" and falls. And again, in the book of Psalms, we are told that the Lord knows full well how the human mind reasons, and how foolish and futile it is.

So don't be proud of following the wise men of this world. For God has already given you everything you need. He has given you Paul and Apollos and Peter as your helpers. He has given you the whole world to use, and life and even death are your servants. He has given you all of the present and all of the future. All are yours, and you belong to Christ, and Christ is God's.

-1 Corinthians 3:10-23

So, we are the temple of God; God's house. God / the Holy Spirit lives inside of us, and, when He moved in, we certainly should have been aware of it … just as when a guest comes into your home to spend time! His Word is the Blueprint to a rich and prosperous life here on this dot. Whatever we may be going through, whatever mountain of problems we may face, we are to go to the Bible for wisdom. This wisdom, God's Word, is built on the One True foundation, and we are to take care in picking out our building materials … inspection will be thorough and rigorous. At the Judgment Seat of Christ, the Master will know and expose any obscurities of the Truth … acts performed for appearances only. Inferior building materials, if you will. How we treat and relate to others is of utmost importance! Everyone's work will be put through the fire so that all can see whether or not it keeps its value, and what was really accomplished. Are my actions of value to eternity? Is God attached to them?

"And if, as my representatives, you give even a cup of cold water to a little child, you will surely be rewarded."

-Matthew 10:42

As representatives of Jesus Christ, Yeshua, we should have a strong desire to be handing out cold water to all little children! The details do matter!

> [O]n that day when, according to my gospel, God judges the secrets of men by Christ Jesus.
>
> -Romans 2:16 ESV

As Christians, as disciples, we should continuously be aware of and focused on our desires and our thoughts ... they will be on the projector as the tape is rolling on Judgment Day. When I handed that bottle of water to that little girl [that human being], what was I thinking? Genuine generosity counts!

> By this time the crowd, unwieldy and stepping on each other's toes, numbered into the thousands. But Jesus' primary concern was his disciples. He said to them, "Watch yourselves carefully so you don't get contaminated with Pharisee yeast, Pharisee phoniness. You can't keep your true self hidden forever; before long you'll be exposed. You can't hide behind a religious mask forever; sooner or later the mask will slip and your true face will be known. You can't whisper one thing in private and preach the opposite in public; the day's coming when those whispers will be repeated all over town.["]
>
> -Luke 12:1-3 MSG

And last, but certainly not least, let's talk about our words ... our daily declarations. Do my words edify others? Do I speak words of life, or words of death? Jesus says:

> ["]A good man's speech reveals the rich treasures within him. An evil-hearted man is filled with venom, and his speech reveals it. And I tell you this, that you must give account on Judgment Day for every idle word you speak. Your words now reflect your fate then:

either you will be justified by them or you will be condemned."

-Matthew 12:35-37

"And I tell you this, that you must give account on Judgment Day for every idle word you speak." Those words, my friend, are straight from the mouth of the Messiah Himself! If you fear the Lord thy God, this means take Him seriously, not casually, this new creature tape that is now recording for playback, starting right this second, should contain as few as possible, careless words. Words that do nothing at all to benefit the Kingdom of God.

So, we have spoken on deeds. We have spoken of desires. And we have spoken of our declarations. All of which are being recorded for Judgment Day. The Good News ... God loves the church! He does not move in our lives proportional to our performance! All that was taken care of on the cross. I would like to propose that we leave this chapter with a new dedication to First Corinthians:

> Don't imagine us leaders to be something we aren't. We are servants of Christ, not his masters. We are guides into God's most sublime secrets, not security guards posted to protect them. The requirements for a good guide are reliability and accurate knowledge. It matters very little to me what you think of me, even less where I rank in popular opinion. I don't even rank myself. Comparisons in these matters are pointless. I'm not aware of anything that would disqualify me from being a good guide for you, but that doesn't mean much. The *Master* makes that judgment.

-1 Corinthians 4:1-4 MSG

As followers of Christ, let's be dependable, not "Christianeeze". If you value the Gift, the price that was paid on that cross, show it! Love. Be kind. Be thankful. Go with God; let's protect His reputation well by way of excellence [useful and fruitful in all things at all times] within our lifestyle. Our God is an awesome God!

Chapter 11
The Interim

We are living in the interim from birth to death. From the year we were born through to the year of our departure from this little bitty dot on a perfect axis in the big ole universe ... the dash on the tombstone if you will!

The Bible reads, Jesus stated, for us to enter into heaven, we have to be born from above, "born again" (*see* John 3:3). Born of the Spirit in order to go and be with the Lord. I propose to us this means so much more than going to the church building plus walking around stating we are Christians. We could put it that Christianity is an exchanged life. We literally turn ourselves over to God. We call Him, "Lord! Lord!" I was one way and now I am another. Salvation is not just an adjustment in our thinking. And it is not changing direction from bad to good. We are new creatures and old things are passed away ... gone. There should be real transformations taking place on the inside of us. Different thinking, going to church, going to Bible study, reading this book ... those kinds of commitments are certainly byproducts of Christianity. And every single solitary person will go to heaven or hell. But when it comes to true Christianity, authentic discipleship, real relationship with God ... God lives on the inside of us. He knows us; every thought, every deed, every emotion, every motive. When we get this new life, we know it. It is heartfelt! It is a heart change with the help of the Holy Spirit!

The evil / wicked / lost are frustrated because they do not yield to, submit to, the help and comfort from the Holy Spirit.

From the heart out, we should have a strong desire to represent the Lord, AND, there should be no reason to *not* look forward to our time to go home or get caught up in the rapture! Is your vision to have relationship?

You see, heaven is a BIG DEAL! All Christians will not enter in the same manner. We all die, cease to exist here ... the heart will eventually stop beating and we will draw our last breath here, or, we will be snatched up at the rapture. Once we become Christians, Christ followers, constantly growing in Christ-LIKE-ness, we are to view our new life with a heavenly perspective ... on earth as it is in heaven.

Drawing the supernatural from the heavens, awaiting an abundant entrance into the heavens.

> And God will open wide the gates of heaven for you to enter into the eternal kingdom of our Lord and Savior Jesus Christ.
>
> -2 Peter 1:11

God's desire is that we live our lives in time from the viewpoint of eternity with Him ... in the eternal kingdom. Our days here on earth, on this tiny dot floating precisely in this big ole universe, are numbered.

> And now, my little children, stay in happy fellowship with the Lord so that when He comes you will be sure that all is well, and will not have to be ashamed and shrink back from meeting him.
>
> -1 John 2:28

There are multiple levels of heaven with many mansions. And, as we are told in this Scripture, some Christians will enter ashamed at His coming. Shrinking away. Embarrassed at this first meeting. Disappointed. At the meeting of the King of kings and Lord of lords who loves the whosoever so much, that He gave His own life so we could have fellowship with Him eternally. However, while we were pilgrims here, He was unable to use us in the growth of the Kingdom. Paul says to the believers of Corinth:

> But, instead, you yourselves are the ones who do wrong, cheating others, even your own brothers.
>
> Don't you know that those doing such things have no share in the Kingdom of God? Don't fool yourselves. Those who live immoral lives, who are idol worshipers, adulterers or homosexuals—will have no share in his Kingdom.   Neither will thieves or greedy people, drunkards, slanderers, or robbers. There was a time when some of you were just like that but now your sins are washed away, and you are set apart for God, and he has accepted you because of what the Lord Jesus Christ and the Spirit of our God have done for you.
>
> -1 Corinthians 6:8-11

Jesus paid it all. And we will all stand before Him one day. Do not be deceived! He does not say that the Christian will not enter heaven. He says those [the Christians who continue of no benefit to God or His Kingdom] will not inherit it. When we transition from here to there, living life with Christ as our foundation, seeking His will for our lives, being of one mind and one accord with Him and with each other, NOT disregarding our FREE salvation, we will enter spectacularly. From glory to glory to glory. Receiving our inheritance as representative of the Risen King. Our rewards, laid up in heaven, for the pure works we have done here, with pure motives and true love for the King. A rich welcome to those of us who chose to stop loving evil pleasures … the evil things of this world that are NOT from God. Those who repent, confess, turn, and renew our minds for Biblical worldviews, Biblical values. Those of us practicing the processes related to bearing good fruit.

Should the Lord come today, or, if today is the last day of our "soon", we should be excited about the level of heaven that we are going to experience! When we choose to live a life that pleases and honors the Lord, we will experience that abundant entrance plus spectacular inheritance.

> Dear children, this world's last hour has come. You have heard about the Antichrist who is coming—the one who is against Christ—and already many such persons have appeared. This makes us all the more certain that the end of the world is near. These "against-Christ" people used to be members of our churches, but they never really belonged with us or else they would have stayed. When they left us it proved that they were not of us at all.
>
> -1 John 2:18-19

"Soon" we shall sit at the Judgment Seat of Christ. We enter and we get to review our tapes … the ones that are currently running … to be judged for our works.

> For we must all stand before Christ to be judged and have our lives laid bare—before him. Each of us will receive whatever he deserves for the good or bad things he has done in his earthly body.
>
> -2 Corinthians 5:10

How does your tape read? Starting right now. Right this second. All will appear, and there will be no stand-ins, no substitutes for ANY man. What is my character? What are my contributions to the Kingdom? What is my conduct during this cultural assault on our Risen King?

> "Again, the Kingdom of Heaven can be illustrated by the story of a man going into another country, who called together his servants and loaned them money to invest for him while he was gone.
>
> He gave $5,000 to one, $2,000 to another, and $1,000 to the last—dividing it in proportion to their abilities—and then left on his trip. The man who received the $5,000 began immediately to buy and sell with it and soon earned another $5,000. The man with $2,000 went right to work, too, and earned another $2,000.
>
> But the man who received the $1,000 dug a hole in the ground and hid the money for safekeeping.
>
> After a long time their master returned from his trip and called them to him to account for his money. The man to whom he entrusted the $5,000 brought him $10,000.
>
> His master praised him for good work. 'You have been faithful in handling this small amount', he told him, 'so now I will give you many more responsibilities. Begin the joyous tasks I have assigned to you.'
>
> Next came the man who had received the $2,000, with the report, 'Sir, you gave me $2,000 to use, and I have doubled it.'

'Good work', his master said. 'You are a good and faithful servant. You have been faithful over this small amount, so now I will give you much more.'

Then the man with the $1,000 came and said, 'Sir, I knew you were a hard man, and I was afraid you would rob me of what I earned, so I hid your money in the earth and here it is!'

But his master replied, 'Wicked man! Lazy slave! Since you knew I would demand your profit, you should at least have put my money into the bank so I could have some interest. Take the money from this man and give it to the man with the $10,000. For the man who uses well what he is given shall be given more, and he shall have abundance. But from the man who is unfaithful, even what little responsibility he has shall be taken from him. And throw the useless servant out into outer darkness: there shall be weeping and gnashing of teeth.'["]

-Matthew 25:14-30

Jesus tells us this parable to illustrate the Kingdom of Heaven. The man goes on a journey, as we are in this moment in time, and he leaves these three different amounts of money with three different servants. He returns after a long time, or "soon", depending on how you want to look at it, and questions all three servants. So, we are sitting at the Seat of Judgement ... and Jesus asks those of us with the $5,000 what we did with the abilities that He gave us ... our heavenly assignments are then decided on ... by THE Judge ... based on rewards for usefulness and fruitfulness. Our works. Those with the many who produced many more will be put over more. Govern, in some capacity, over cities.

Those of us who receive the $2,000 and earn another $2,000, will also be ruled upon rightly and given his or her assignment.

But, what about the servant of God ... the man, woman, child of God ... who received $1,000? With the ability to sing? With the ability to preach? With the ability to help others? Who chose to bury their God-given talents and abilities in a hole? You see, God does not expect those of us who have one talent to do as those of us who have various gifts. Only to do that which He has given us, those divine abilities specifically God-given to the individual. Those of us who "play it safe". In other words, if Jesus does not return, 'I got the money'. If the Master does return, I can show Him that I still have the money. That I did not lose it [kept it hidden, all to myself]. Well, we will hear 'Wicked man! Lazy slave!' Here in lies the "shrinking away." The reason we choose not to put the money in the bank to AT LEAST draw interest is because banks keep records and we do not want a record of what we are doing. Our deeds on the tape of our impure desires, our impure declarations, our impure works, our impure contributions.

> [']For to everyone who has will more be given, and he will have an abundance. But from the one who has not, even what he has will be taken away. And cast the worthless servant into the outer darkness. In that place there will be weeping and gnashing of teeth.'
>
> -Matthew 25:29-30 ESV

When we meet our Master, our faithfulness and pure deeds are rewarded through assignment—the useless and the fruitless as well. Our heavenly experiences are assigned at the review by our Master. Faithful and useful disciples will be appointed to our places in the heavens where there will be multilevel experiences in the perfect, celestial body. And, until we arrive, we are unaware of the actual sensations we will experience in that glorified body. We can only imagine. We are all forgiven sinners. Our High Priest is in heaven and seated at the place of highest honor, quite literally next to God Himself. And He is appointed to judge and reward His servants. Sensations experienced in heaven by saints cannot be measured here on earth while our spirit lives in the physical body. If sin grieves a perfect God, saints, surely just as angels, will also have sensations ... experience sensations in our glorified body. There is a substantial difference between salvation and discipleship. Salvation comes free in the finished work of Christ, and it is offered, available to the whosoever. Discipleship comes with the cost of standing up to cultural assault. Swimming upstream. God's ways are not our ways. Choosing Christ, choosing discipleship, choosing an intimate, personal relationship with the Holy Spirit, is serious business. It is living life as a full-time servant.

> Here is my final conclusion: fear God and obey His commandments, for this is the entire duty of man. For God will judge us for everything we do, including every hidden thing, good or bad.
> -Ecclesiastes 12:13-14

Praise God, while we are still here, we are on tape. The tape that Christ will review at the Judgment when our heavenly assignments in our glorified bodies are distributed.

> And remember that your heavenly Father to whom you pray has no favorites when he judges. He will judge you with perfect justice for everything you do; so act in reverent fear of Him from now on until you get to heaven. God paid a ransom to save you from the impossible road to heaven which your fathers tried to

take, and the ransom He paid was not mere gold or silver, as you very well know. But he paid for you with the precious lifeblood of Christ, the sinless, spotless Lamb of God.

-1 Peter 1:17-19

Long before the dot, this world began. All Christians have the exact same opportunity to enter heaven abundantly.

Long ago, even before he made the world, God chose us to be his very own through what Christ would do for us; he decided then to make us holy in his eyes, without a single fault—we who stand before him covered with his love. His unchanging plan has always been to adopt us into his own family by sending Jesus Christ to die for us. And he did this because he wanted to!

-Ephesians 1:4-5

His plans have not changed. His love is undeserved and unconditional.

And let us not get tired of doing what is right, for after a while we will reap a harvest of blessing if we don't get discouraged and give up. That's why whenever we can we should always be kind to everyone, and especially to our Christian brothers.

-Galatians 6:9-10

Let's ask ourselves, what are my priorities? What do I make time for? Do I seek Him first?

[A]nd he will give them to you if you give him first place in your life and live as he wants you to.

-Matthew 6:33

Or, is this little bitty dot, floating precisely in this big ole universe, with all kinds of cultural assaults, more important to me? In other words, is the eternal more important to us than this temporal [the things of this world]? Do we do the dot from the perspective of eternity? Operating here and now, relationing with the Holy Spirit in control, by investing in there. The Holy Spirit is who can get us through the now. This Spirit of God, on the inside of every Christian awaits our willingness, our acceptance, our conformity, our submission to discipleship for Christ to become useful and fruitful. Then, immense rewards in the heavens! Disciples are willing to make adjustments in our lives, according to the will of God for our lives, since we believe in the life to come. Plus, we truly desire, we are diligent to receive, more of His presence in the life that is right now, on this teeny tiny dot, strategically placed, in this big ole universe full with the Love of God, holding faithful to peace during the cultural assault of evil deeds and evil-doers ... satan's playground of over 8 billion minds feeding over 8 billion hearts which are currently beating until the completion of this journey through this world.

Yeshua sacrificed Himself, God gave His only begotten Son, on the cross for reconciliation ... making something new. We are reconciled through the Blood. And this new relationship is to be the starting point for everything else in our experiences in the Christian life. Otherwise, how can we expect trans-formation in culture?

Once we are redeemed by Christ, forgiven by God, in the process of being transformed with the help of the Holy Spirit, we are new in Christ, sharing the same faith ... belonging to the same church [temple] ... one body. No more Jew or

Gentile. No more circumcised or uncircumcised. We are to be Christian first.

> Now because of Christ—dying that death, shedding that blood—you who were once out of it altogether are in on everything.
>
> The Messiah has made things up between us so that we're now together on this, both non-Jewish outsiders and Jewish insiders. He tore down the wall we used to keep each other at a distance. He repealed the law code that had become so clogged with fine print and footnotes that it hindered more than it helped. Then he started over. Instead of continuing with two groups of people separated by centuries of animosity and suspicion, he created a new kind of human being, a fresh start for everybody.
>
> Christ brought us together through his death on the cross. The cross got us to embrace, and that was the end of the hostility. Christ came and preached peace to you outsiders and peace to us insiders. He treated us as equals, and so made us equals. Through him we both share the same Spirit and have equal access to the Father.
>
> That's plain enough, isn't it? You're no longer wandering exiles. This kingdom of faith is now your home country. You're no longer strangers or outsiders. You belong here, with as much right to the name Christian as anyone. God is building a home. He's using us all—irrespective of how we got here—in what he is building. He used the apostles and prophets for the foundation. Now he's using you, fitting you in brick by brick, stone by stone, with Christ Jesus as the cornerstone that holds all the parts together. We see it taking shape day

after day—a holy temple built by God, all of us built into it, a temple in which God is quite at home.

-Ephesians 2:13-22 MSG

Let's not be confined [imprisoned] to yesterday [the old, the past, the familiar]. It keeps us locked up, chained up, in our normal way of labeling. When we appeal to the Word of God and God's people can get it right, _then_ we have some Good News to offer the culture.

And this reason? To show to all the rulers in heaven how perfectly wise he is when all of his family—Jews and Gentiles alike—are seen to be joined together in his Church in just the way he had always planned it through Jesus Christ our Lord.

Now we can come fearlessly right into God's presence, assured of his glad welcome when we come with Christ and trust in him.

-Ephesians 3:10-12

From now on, therefore, we regard no one according to the flesh. Even though we once regarded Christ according to the flesh, we regard him thus no longer. Therefore, if anyone is in Christ, he is a new creation. The old has passed away; behold, the new has come. All this is from God, who through Christ reconciled us to himself and gave us the ministry of reconciliation; that is, in Christ God was reconciling the world to himself, not counting their trespasses against them, and entrusting to us the message of reconciliation.

-2 Corinthians 5:16-19 ESV

Let's give 'em something else to talk about!

Chapter 12
The Conclusion

Faith and family are under attack ... there is a cultural assault on our children and our grandchildren. We are living in a secular, media-saturated time preceded like no other. Video games and cell phones with internet and social platforms expose competitions and comparisons and insecurities, all hostile to the Biblical faith, are not only immediately accessible, but growingly fed to our younger generations as some sort of pacifier ... to satisfy and occupy their minds and time so that parents don't have to deal with crying or distress or discipline. satan is working relentlessly to capture their hearts and minds through their physical eyesights and fickle emotions. Suicides and entitlement and labeling and a blatant denial of the Creator and addictions to try and help numb realities are at an all-time high ... out of control.

Keeping God's Word, Biblical values, a Biblical worldview, fresh and alive before us, in the lives of our children, is vitally important. More so than ever before! Otherwise, evil will abound evermore abundantly, negatively affect the upcoming leaders of *this* world, and continue to contribute in keeping us captive in our real, born into, human-nature, morally wrong, sinful creatures that we are [before our new birth]. And so, there begins the problems, the circling of the mountains. Over and over, again and again!

The Good News, the two choices: We can serve and please God (LIFE), or, we can serve and please self (DEATH). However, rest assured, God will never, never, never, violate our free will.

Human suffering is inevitable. Just take the time to research what Jesus Christ, the real person, in human flesh, suffered so that whosoever can be reconciled with God. There is no program or pill or president who can offer the elimination of suffering. Labeling only contributes to the Exile into Babylon story found within the Bible. If we insist on playing the blame-game, blaming God for everything evil, reducing God to something we can control or use when we need something, we do not know God at all. Nor do we understand human nature. And there are consequences. Suffering is an unavoidable element when living on this dot, this fallen earth. The Scriptures, God's Word, provides us with the history of suffering and labeling and pride and God's judgment ... and redemption!

Our community of faith, the one-body of Christ-like faith, chooses God's Word as the Survival Guide for dealing with loss and pain for victory and freedom. We believe and we receive that God is with us, God is in us, God is for us, and God is our companion and friend through **_all_** things. We know, that we know, that we know, that GREAT is God's faithfulness, life is a wonderful gift from God, by God, and about relationship with God, in Jesus Christ, and that heaven is a big deal. It is the place where we will share space and eternity in the presence of God.

There are many lessons we can all take to heart from the Book of Lamentations. They too were experiencing life on this tiny little dot, floating flawlessly in God's big ole universe. It is perfectly fine to cry out to God in prayer, and then turn to Him in trust. God will never, never, never, let us down!

> *Yes there is one ray of hope: his compassion never ends.* It is only the Lord's mercies that have kept us from complete destruction. Great is his faithfulness; his

loving kindness begins afresh each day. My soul claims the Lord as my inheritance; therefore I will hope in him. The Lord is wonderfully good to those who wait for him, to those who seek for him. It is good both to hope and wait quietly for the salvation of the Lord.

It is good for a young man to be under discipline, for it causes him to sit apart in silence beneath the Lord's demands, to lie face downward in the dust; then at last there is hope for him. Let him turn the other cheek to those who strike him and accept their awful insults, for the Lord will not abandon him forever. Although God gives him grief, yet he will show compassion too, according to the greatness of his lovingkindness. For he does not enjoy afflicting men and causing sorrow.

But you have trampled and crushed beneath your feet the lowly of the world, and deprived men of their God-given rights, and refused them justice. No wonder the Lord has had to deal with you! For who can act against you without the Lord's permission? It is the Lord who helps one and harms another.

Why then should we, mere humans as we are, murmur and complain when punished for our sins? Let us examine ourselves instead, and repent and turn again to the Lord. Let us lift our hearts and hands to him in heaven, for we have sinned; we have rebelled against the Lord, and he has not forgotten it.

You have engulfed us by your anger, Lord, and slain us without mercy. You have veiled yourself as with a cloud so that our prayers do not reach through. You have made us as refuse and garbage among the nations. All our enemies have spoken out against us. We are filled with fear, for we are trapped and desolate, destroyed.

My eyes flow day and night with never-ending streams of tears because of the destruction of my people. Oh, that the Lord might look down from heaven and respond to my cry! My heart is breaking over what is happening to the young girls of Jerusalem.

My enemies, whom I have never harmed, chased me as though I were a bird. They threw me in a well and capped it with a rock. The water flowed above my head. I thought, This is the end! But I called upon your name, O Lord, from deep within the well, and you heard me! You listen to my pleading; you heard my weeping! Yes, you came at my despairing cry and told me not to fear.

O Lord, you are my lawyer! Plead my case! For you have redeemed my life. You have seen the wrong they did to me; be my Judge, to prove me right. You have seen the plots my foes have laid against me. You have heard the vile names they have called me, and all they say about me and their whispered plans. See how they laugh and sing with glee, preparing my doom.

O Lord, repay them well for all the evil they have done. Harden their hearts and curse them, Lord. Go after them in fierce pursuit and wipe them off the earth, beneath the heavens of the Lord.

-Lamentations 3:21-66

Below, is the same Passage of Scripture from the AMPC translation of the Bible. I included cross reference verses for deeper study.

But this I recall and therefore have I hope *and* expectation:

It is because of the Lord's mercy *and* loving-kindness that we are not consumed, because His [tender] compassions fail not. [Malachi 3:6]

They are new every morning; great *and* abundant is Your stability *and* faithfulness. [Isaiah 33:2]

The Lord is my portion *or* share, says my living being (my inner self); therefore will I hope in Him *and* wait expectantly for Him. [Numbers 18:20]

The Lord is good to those who wait hopefully *and* expectantly for Him, to those who seek Him [inquire of and for Him and require Him by right of necessity and on the authority of God's word].

It is good that one should hope in *and* wait quietly for the salvation (the safety and ease) of the Lord.

It is good for a man that he should bear the yoke [of divine disciplinary dealings] in his youth.

Let him sit alone uncomplaining *and* keeping silent [in hope], because [God] has laid [the yoke] upon him [for his benefit]. [Romans 8:28]

Let him put his mouth in the dust [in abject recognition of his unworthiness]—there may yet be hope. [Micah 7:17]

Let him give his cheek to the One Who smites him [even through His human agents]; let him be filled [full] with [men's] reproach [in meekness].

For the Lord will not cast off forever! [Psalm 94:14]

But though He causes grief, yet will He be moved to compassion according to the multitude of His loving-kindness *and* tender mercy.

For He does not willingly *and* from His heart afflict or grieve the children of men. [Ezekiel 18:23, 32; Hosea 11:8; Hebrews 12:5-10; 2 Peter 3:9]

To trample *and* crush underfoot all the prisoners of the earth,

To turn aside *and* deprive a man of his rights before the face of the Most High *or* a superior [acting as God's representative],

To subvert a man in his cause—[of these things] the Lord does not approve.

Who is he who speaks and it comes to pass, if the Lord has not authorized *and* commanded it?

Is it not out of the mouth of the Most High that evil and good both proceed [adversity and prosperity, physical evil or misfortune and physical good or happiness]?

Why does a living man sigh [one who is still in this life's school of discipline]? [And why does] a man complain for the punishment of his sins?

Let us test and examine our ways, and let us return to the Lord!

Let us lift up our hearts and our hands [and then with them mount up in prayer] to God in heaven:

We have transgressed and rebelled and You have not pardoned.

You have covered Yourself with wrath and pursued *and* afflicted us; You have slain without pity.

You have covered Yourself with a cloud so that no prayer can pass through.

You have made us offscouring and refuse among the nations.

All our enemies have gaped at us *and* railed against us.

Fear and pitfall have come upon us, devastation and destruction.

My eyes overflow with streams of tears because of the destruction of the daughter of my people.

My eyes overflow continually and will not cease

Until the Lord looks down and sees from heaven.

My eyes cause me grief at the fate of all the maidens [and the daughter-towns] of my city [Jerusalem].

I have been hunted down like a bird by those who were my enemies without cause.

They [thought they had] destroyed my life in the dungeon (pit) and cast a stone [over it] above me.

The waters ran down on my head; I said, I am gone.

I called upon Your name, O Lord, out of the depths [of the mire] of the dungeon.

You heard my voice [then]: [Oh] hide not Your ear [now] at my prayer for relief.

You drew near on the day I called to You; You said, Fear not.

O Lord, You have pleaded the causes of my soul [You have managed my affairs and You have protected my person and my rights]; You have rescued *and* redeemed my life!

O Lord, You have seen my wrong [done to me]; judge *and* maintain my cause.

You have seen all their vengeance, all their devices against me.

You have heard their reproach *and* revilings, O Lord, and all their devices against me—

The lips *and* thoughts of my assailants are against me all day long.

Look at their sitting down and their rising up [their movements, doings, and secret counsels]; I am their singsong [the subject of their derision and merriment].

Render to them a recompense, O Lord, according to the work of their hands.

You will give them hardness *and* blindness of heart; Your curse will be upon them.

You will pursue *and* afflict them in anger and destroy them from under Your heavens, O Lord.

-Lamentations 3:21-66 AMPC

About the Author

Drugs and alcohol and men and manipulation were the driving forces throughout my 20+ years in Downtown Atlanta, Georgia. I am now a living testament that our God is a big-ole, awesome GOD! Ain't it awesome that we can call out to the Lord! I am so thankful He has put this, His still small voice, on the inside of my conscience, that speaks to me ever so gently. Once I learned religion and relationship are not the same thing, my relationship with God has truly transformed me, AND, He is available to the whosoever!

It was in a drunken stupor I passed out one night a few years back. Then, the Lord woke me and said, "My child, you need to follow Me." Understand, I was living my life "taking His name in vain". From that moment, and to this day, I was healed. The Bible reads, once unbeknown to me, that we are one spirit with Christ. That we are spirit, soul, and body. In my continuing education in the Word of God, which I like to refer to as our Survival Guide, I have come to know that means, in my spirit, I am one with Christ. Plus, Abba Father sees all His chosen children, through His eyes, just as He sees His Son! My responsibility, our responsibility, is to also see His Word as our mirror ... to see ourselves the same way. Once I got ahold of the difference between "fleshly" and "spiritually", God could better deal with me, deep down inside my heart and soul, that our spirits are one, and that is it was my body and mind which needed the transformation.

Renewal of the mind with the mirror of Christ is crucial. Christ's sacrifice paid it all. No renewal, no new thoughts that line up with the character of Christ. No new actions, no new creature taken over by the Holy Spirit of Christ, so to act and react by / within the standards of God. The Word of God should set our standards. Be our point of conscience [set the boundaries of our conscience]. That is why God chose us as part of His family … to glorify Him. He is the way. His ways are better and higher. His convictions and His love work together, inside of us, and, when we disconnect, get out of sync, it is oh-so-easy to lose our footing [lose our way].

Walking, step-by-step, side-by-side, with God, with God's Spirit, is a privilege! My intentional sin is my choice & my unintentional sin is forgiven! Our walk with the Spirit leads us not into temptation AND delivers us from evil. His Will is all based on His Word. To know "about" is one thing. To "know" is a whole other thing. Dependance on the Spirit is crucial so that the Father is able to work all things out for good to those of us who truly love Him and live a lifestyle according to His Word. We are saved by trusting. God knows our conditions. And, we can be victorious WITH / IN HIM. Sometimes, human's focus on the evil takes our focus off the good. God answers prayers according to His Will. God providentially arranges things. By means of God's providence. His act of providing or preparing for future use or application. His foresight. His timely care. His care and superintendence which HE, God, exercises over His creatures … great and small. Procured beforehand … prior to DAY 1. He foresees our wants and needs. In all things. Through all things. Divine, Trinity, Providence! God is alive & well. And, because He works within His laws to stitch things together to accomplish His sovereign goal, when we keep Him FIRST, providence is what He uses to accomplish His Goal.

I have truly realized … God doesn't need me, I need HIM. He chose me. And now, I have chosen Him. To love God means to passionately pursue His glory. And, once I turned it ALL over to Him, I am truly His. Progressively, I allow Him to be and affect every part of my being including my emotions, my spirit, and my physical strength. Who the Son sets free, she / he / we are free indeed.

During my cooperation with the Spirit of the Son, He, through me, has published two books, *Guilty If Arrested* and this one, *God Will Never Violate Your Free Will*. He has allowed me to host Bible study in my home since February 2023 and has given a Tuesday night ministry for ladies to me, which began January 2025. His Spirit leads [prompts] me to do live YouTube broadcasts.

@kymdavis9583

One of the things I enjoy most, I love most, in my new relationship with God, my getting better and better, more and more, relationship with the Holy Spirit of God, is the revelations and experiences we share as we journey through this adventure here, together. On this, our journey, together, into our eternity, together! Him in me & I in He! Me, allowing Him to lead me down this narrow path that involves communication [2-way conversation], and trust [trust goes both ways], and obedience. Obedience is my obligation, and my choice. His Spirit stimulating mine in all things. Transformation IS available. Trust me. I am living proof of our LIVING GOD.

www.ingramcontent.com/pod-product-compliance
Lightning Source LLC
Chambersburg PA
CBHW061657120626
46550CB00003B/978